The World in a Nutshell

Israel

in a nutshell

*

Enisen Publishing

Israel in a Nutshell

*The founders of Israel adopted the Zionist flag in October 1948 to be the official flag of the State of Israel. The flag has a white background with two sky-blue stripes along the margins. In the center, between the two stripes, is a hexagon or six-pointed star called the Star of David. The white background symbolizes spiritual purity. The blue stripes were inspired by the stripes on the *tallit* (a Jewish prayer shawl) fashioned to reflect holy references in the Torah (Judaism's holy book) to the "color of the sky" (the staff of the prophet Aaron [Moses' brother] was believed to be blue, for example as were the Tablets of the Law). The Star of David , which originally had no religious meaning, was first used to identify the Jewish community in the 19th century and gained a very powerful connotation as a result of abuse of the symbol by Nazis before and during World War II.

*****

Note: This book uses the initials B.C. ("before Christ") and A.D. ("Anno Domini" or "in the year of the Lord") rather than B.C.E. ("Before the Common Era") and C.E. (in the "Common Era") to designate years since the writer and editors felt these terms were most familiar to Nutshell Notes readers.

*****

We understand that future activities may modify or shed new light on some of the data in this book. For that reason, Nutshell Notes, L.L.C. and Enisen Publishing invite readers to visit our website www.nutshellnotes.com to learn about the latest developments concerning Israel/Palestine.

Special Thanks to:
Professor Michael Meyer
and Terry Abrahamian

Israel/Palestine
First edition - January 2004
First published - January 2004

Enisen Publishing
2118 Wilshire Boulevard, #351
Santa Monica, Ca 90403-5784
(866) ENISENP 866-364-7367
http://www.enisen.com
publishing@enisen.com
aroraback@msn.com

Text	Amanda Roraback
Maps	Katie Gerber
Cover design	C.W. Herlong
Editor-in-Chief	Dorothy Roraback
Asst. Editor	Paul Bernhard

ISBN #0-9702908-4-5

Printed in the United States of America

TABLE OF CONTENTS

ISRAEL/PALESTINE AT A GLANCE

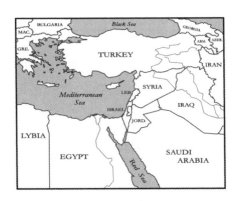

The Region at a Glance

FACTS AND FIGURES

Capital City: Jerusalem (note: Israel proclaimed Jerusalem as its capital in 1950, but the U.S., like nearly all other countries, maintains its embassy in Tel Aviv.

Area 12,900 sq. mi.

Head of Government: Ariel Sharon (since March 2001)

Chief of State: President Moshe Katsav (since July 2000) (next election 2007)

Government Type: parliamentary democracy

Legislative branch: Knesset or parliament (120 seats)

Primary Political Parties: Likud, Labor, Shinui, Shas, National Union

Independence: May 14, 1948

Population: 6,116,533 (note: includes about 187,000 Israeli settlers in the West Bank, about 20,000 in the Israeli-occupied Golan Heights, more than 5,000 in the Gaza Strip, and fewer than 177,000 in East Jerusalem)

Age structure: 0-14 years 26.9%, 15-64 years: 63.2%, 65 years and over: 9.9%   median age, total 28.9 yrs.

Population growth rate: 1.36%

Total fertility rate: 2.5 children born per woman (2003 est.)

Religions: Jewish 80.1%, Muslim 14.6% (mostly Sunni Muslim), Christian 2.1%, other 3.2% (1996 est.)

Languages: Hebrew (official), Arabic

Literacy: Total pop. 95.4%, male 97.3%, female 93.6%

Currency: New Israeli shekel

GDP (per capita): $19,000 (2002 est.)

Pop. below the poverty line: 18% (2001 est.)

Unemployment rate: 10.4% (2002 est.)

Airports: 52 (Railways: 640 km)

Telephones: 2.8 million (main lines) 2.5 million (cellular)

Military Branches: Israel Defense Forces(IDF),Pioneer Fighting Youth (Shabak or Shin Bet -- domestic security agency)

Military manpower avail.: males age 15-49, 1,562,716, females 15-49, 1,516,505 (both sexes liable for military service)

Military expenditures: $8.97 billion (FY02) (8.72% of GDP)

Figures taken from the CIA World Factbook 2003

TERMS

Eretz-Israel
The Land of Israel

Zionism
The word "Zion" refers to the hill in Jerusalem captured by the second king of the Israelites, David, and made the site of his royal palace. The word was later used to denote Jerusalem in general and then Israel. "Zionists" are dedicated to restoring "Zion" as a spiritual and political center for the Jewish people.

Aliyah
Meaning "to go up" in Hebrew, the word *aliyah* is applied to Jewish immigration into Israel. The word *yeridah* meaning "to go down" refers to emigration from Israel.

Sephardim
Descendants of Jews from Spain and Portugal. After being expelled from Spain in the late 15th century, most Sephardic Jews resettled in Arab-Muslim countries. Sephardic Jews spoke a hybrid Hebrew-Spanish language called Ladino. The word "Sephardic" is derived from the Hebrew word for Spain.

Ashkenazim
Jews originating from Central and Eastern Europe (Poland, Germany, Lithuania) and their descendants. Most Ashkenazim (from the Hebrew word "Ashkenaz" referring to the area roughly corresponding to Germany) spoke Yiddish (a combination of Hebrew and medieval German) and followed Ashkenzic traditions. Most Jews today are Ashkenzic.

Mandate
Commission assigned by the League of Nations after World War I giving European powers the authority to command territories surrendered by Turkey and Germany until the inhabitants were able to govern themselves.

David Ben-Gurion
Ben-Gurion proclaimed Israel's independence on May 14, 1948 (Israeli Independence Day) and became the new nation's first prime minister.

Knesset
Israeli parliament

Labor (Labour)Party
Israeli political party formed by a union of three left-of-center socialist parties. The Labor Party dominated Israeli politics until 1977.

Likud (Union) Party
Right-of-center Israeli political party that emerged in 1977 with the election of Menachim Begin. Likud Party members generally support the construction and maintenance of Israeli settlements in Gaza and the West Bank.

IDF (Israeli Defense Force)
Israel's army. All Israelis (male and female) are required to serve in the IDF at

the age of 18 for a compulsory three year term for men, and 18-month term for women.

Outposts/Settlements
"Settlements" are new Israeli communities built on territories captured after the 1967 Arab-Israeli War (in the West Bank and Gaza Strip). "Outposts" are the "seeds" of future settlements beginning as small parcels of land on Palestinian-populated territory. The land is sometimes acquired by the Israeli government for government use (as a site for a telephone line, an industrial park, water tower, etc.) or claimed by small groups of Israelis (even a single family or individual) living in trailers or other temporary homes.

Fact on the Ground
Term used to describe the establishment of a settlement in the West Bank and Gaza Strip. The settlements act as Israeli claims to land within historic Israel making it difficult for the transfer of territory to the Palestinians.

Green Line
Imaginary line demarcating the borders between Israel and the West Bank and Gaza Strip as recognized by the international community. Its proper name is the "1949 Armistice Line."

Separation Wall
Wall built under the direction of Ariel Sharon along the *green line* as a barrier between Israeli and Palestinian territories. The wall was commissioned after a wave of Palestinian suicide bombings in 2002 in order to prevent future terrorist incursions into Israel. (Cost - approx. $1 million per mile)

Torah
The word "Torah" refers both to the first five books of the Hebrew Scriptures (also called the "Pentateuch") and the entire Hebrew Bible or "Tanakh" (considered the "Old Testament" to Christians). The Torah includes the books given directly to Moses by God, the "Prophets" or books written by saintly people who communicated with God, and "writings" written by prophets under God's guidance.

Talmud
A compilation of books containing messages and lessons passed orally from Moses to religious leaders (called the *Mishna* or "tradition") and analyses and commentaries on the Mishna (compiled in the *Gemara* or "completion"). The Talmud includes rules on religious practice (prayer, observation of the Shabbath, ritual cleansing etc.) and laws regarding daily life (agriculture, marriage, divorce, civil and criminal laws etc.)

Judea and Samaria
Historical parts of *Eretz-Israel* (the Land of Israel) west of the Jordan River. The area has been popularly called the "West Bank" since Jordan overran the territory in 1948.

BIBLICAL HISTORY

As told in the first books of the **Torah** (the Old Testament), the story of *Eretz-Israel* (the "land of Israel") begins around 1800 B.C. in the town of Ur (in present-day Iraq) with a command and a promise from God to a man called **Abraham**. At the age of 75, Abraham was instructed to leave the land of his father with his wife **Sarah** to populate a land where his people could worship God. In return, God promised that Abraham would have many, many descendants – even though Sarah was barren and long past her childbearing years.

After a period of enslavement and affliction that would last for 400 years, Abraham's descendants, God's "Chosen People," would inherit the land of **Canaan** from the Nile River (in Egypt) to the Euphrates River (in present-day Iraq) for the rest of time. (Genesis 17:1-8).

As God had commanded, Abraham traveled to **Mount Moriah** in Jerusalem (the future site of the **Temple Mount**) where, in order to facilitate God's promise of a nation created from Abraham's offspring, Sarah convinced Abraham to be intimate with her Egyptian slave, **Hagar**. Hagar bore Abraham a son called **Ishmael**.

Soon after, though, Sarah, at the age of 90-years, bore Abraham a son of her own who was called **Isaac** and was circumcised eight days after his birth in accordance with God's will. Although she was the one who had suggested Abraham's liaison with Hagar, Sarah became jealous and fearful of Abraham's older son, Ishmael, and asked her husband to send mother and child away into the desert(Muslims believe that they are the descendants of Ishmael who was outcast with his mother to Mecca in present-day Saudi Arabia). (See "Abraham" in Palestine section)

As a test of Abraham's devotion and trust, God presented Abraham with another command - to sacrifice his beloved son, Isaac, on top of Mount Moriah. Just as Abraham's knife was about to cause a fatal wound, however, God, satisfied with Abraham's extreme demonstration of loyalty, stopped him. Isaac, saved from death, eventually grew up to father two sons, **Esau** and **Jacob**.

Of the two, God favored Jacob and called him "**Israel**," meaning "to strive with God and prevail." It was Jacob's twelve sons who eventually became the patriarchs of the twelve tribes of Israel (called the "Hebrew Tribes").

One of Jacob's sons, Joseph, was sold into slavery to merchants on their way to Egypt by his jealous brothers. In Egypt, Joseph won the trust of the Pharaoh and was appointed his minister to rule over the land. When famine hit the land of Canaan, Joseph's brothers joined him with their families.

After Joseph's death, **Rameses II** became Pharaoh and, fearful of their rapid rate of procreation, enslaved the Israelites. Upon hearing a rumor that a deliverer would be born to the Israelites, he ordered that all babies born to the servile group be killed. But one child escaped his death sentence when his mother placed him in a basket and sent him floating down a river.

The Pharaoh's daughter found the child and claimed him as her own. The baby, who was given the Egyptian name, **Moses**, became a prince of Egypt (circa

1350 B.C.).

Moses, who had been chosen by God to deliver the "chosen people" from Egyptian slavery, finally persuaded the Pharaoh to "let his people go" after Egypt suffered divinely-sent plagues. Pursued by the Pharaoh's army, Moses led his people across the Sea of Reeds[1] into Sinai. The Israelites were able to escape the approaching Egyptian forces when God gave Moses the power to separate the waters. After the Hebrews passed through safely, the sea closed again drowning the Egyptian soldiers. For the next 40 years, the people of Israel wandered through the desert on their way back to the land promised to Abraham.

In the course of their journey, the Israelites camped at the foot of Mount Sinai where Moses received an order from God to worship no other god but God, himself. At this time, God also presented Moses with ten commandments inscribed on two stone tablets to be observed by all Israelite people and taught him the laws governing religious observance (compiled in the **Torah**). The Israelites placed a record of the laws and the tablets in a case called the **Ark of the Covenant** and carried it with them as they travelled through the desert.

After four hundred years living in a foreign land and forty years wandering in the desert, the Israelites were finally led back into *Eretz-Israel* by Moses' assistant, Joshua. Once they re-conquered Canaan from the indigenous population, the land was divided among the Israeli tribes.

In order to defend themselves from attacks by the **Philistines** (Sea People who had settled in the coastal areas), the twelve tribes united under the Israelite's first king, **Saul**, from the tribe of Benjamin. Under the command of Saul's son-in-law, **David**, who had succeeded Saul after his death, Jerusalem was captured from the Canaanites and made the Israeli capital. After the Philistines were defeated, David's rich empire was expanded to the Euphrates River in the north and the borders of Sinai in the south.

David's son, **Solomon**, launched an ambitious building program that included constructing a holy **Temple** that would become the new home for the sacred Ark of the Covenant. This period (known in Jewish history as the **First Temple Period**) was marked by expansion, trade and development. Resentment over heavy taxes levied against the Israelites to pay for Solomon's extensive projects as well as jealousies among the tribes finally led to the empire's split into a northern Kingdom of **Israel** (with is capital at Samaria) and a southern kingdom of **Judah** which incorporated the holy city of Jerusalem.

Weakened by the disintegration of the empire, the northern House of Israel was easily conquered by the **Assyrians** in 722 B.C.. The inhabitants of the kingdom were exiled by the victors and scattered all over the world. The "**Ten Lost Tribes**" as they came to be called, so thoroughly assimilated into their foreign habitats that they virtually disappeared from the pages of history.

In the south, the two remaining tribes of the house of **Judah** and **Benjamin**, were spared from exile because they submitted to the Assyrians. They continued to live peacefully in the Kingdom of Judah (later known as Judea under the Romans) for the next 150 years until the **Babylonians**, under command of

---

[1] Sometimes mistaken as the Red Sea.

Israel in a Nutshell

Nebuchadnezzar conquered the Assyrians and forced the Israelites to leave Jerusalem and resettle in Babylon (in present-day Iraq). Nebuchadnezzar then destroyed Jerusalem and ordered his soldiers to burn Solomon's Temple to the ground.

Rather than bringing an end to the Israelite people and their monotheistic beliefs, though, the tragic loss of the temple and the **Babylonian Captivity** inspired the **Jehudim** (people of Judah or "Jews") to reexamine and strengthen their culture. Judaism in captivity enjoyed a period of spiritual growth.

While conditions were tolerable in Babylon, the cultural capital of the world at that time and the land of Abraham's birth, the site of the Garden of Eden, the Tower of Babel and the Hanging Gardens, the Jews yearned to return to their homeland. In a solemn pledge the Jews promised *If I forget thee o Jerusalem, let my right hand forget her cunning. If I do not remember thee, let my tongue cleave to the roof of my mouth: if I prefer not Jerusalem above my chief joy.* (Psalms 137:5-6). To reinforce their pledge, all prayers were directed toward Jerusalem (a practice that continues today).

During the Israelites seventy years in captivity, the image of God became more abstract and the law more universal. The Jewish god, **Yahweh**, was no longer seen as the god of a nation but as the god of mankind who could be worshiped from any point on earth.

Without a central temple, moreover, the Jews congregated at common gathering places (*Synagogues*) to worship God and ritualistic customs associated with the Temple (animal sacrifices, for example) were abandoned.

It was during this time that the Israelites decided to compile all the traditions, legends and laws into a full library that would become the **Torah** (the Bible) and await a Messiah (a savior sent by God and descended from the house of David) who would restore the nation of Israel and redeem the Jewish people.

When Persian **King Cyrus**, a friend to the Jews, conquered Babylon in 537 B.C., he let the Israelites return to Jerusalem to restore the Temple (ushering in the **Second Temple Period**) and rebuild the city -- although some Jews stayed behind to become successful merchants and to develop a center of Jewish culture in Babylon.

For a couple of centuries the Jews lived in peace in *Eretz-Israel* until the Persians were defeated by a Greek force under **Alexander the Great** (356-323 B.C.).

***

Shavuot -- Jewish holiday commemorating God's presentation of the Torah to Moses at Mount Sinai.

Pesach (Passover) -- "Passover" refers to the fact that God "passed over" the houses of the Jews when he was slaying the firstborn of Egypt during the final of the divinely-sent plagues. The day is celebrated by eating only unleavened bread commemorating the fact that the Jews left Egypt in such a hurry that they did not have time to let their bread rise.

Sukkot (booths)
On this holiday Jews live in temporary dwellings to commemorate the 40-year period the Israelis spent wandering in the desert.

GRECO-ROMAN PERIOD

While under the protection of the Persians, the pacifist Jews had no reason to build a military force. When **Alexander the Great** s Greek forces marched through Jerusalem in 331 B.C. therefore, the Jews had no other recourse but to submit to the invaders. For the next nine centuries, therefore, **Judah** became a province of the Greco-Roman Empire.

After Alexander's death, the Greek emperor's vast Empire was divided among his generals. General **Seleucus** controlled Syria and Asia Minor, **Antigonus** ruled Greece and General **Ptolemy** was granted Egypt and Palestine.

The Jews and their new overlords, the **Ptolemies**, enjoyed a relationship of mutual admiration. The Greeks respected Jews for their discipline, laws and concept of God, while the Jews were enamored of Greek philosophy, science and literature. As long as the Jewish subjects paid their nominal tax to the Greek government, moreover, they were freely allowed to practice their own religion.

The **Seleucids**, who defeated the Ptolemies in 198 B.C. and occupied Judah, were not so accommodating. Jerusalem, with its rich Temple[2] and valuable synagogues, was seen as a source of great wealth to the new rulers and the Jewish religion was perceived as an obstacle to Alexander the Great's vision of an empire united by a single culture and a single religion. Like his predecessors, Seleucid Emperor **Antiochus IV Epiphanes** (175-163 B.C.), considered **Hellenism** (as Greek culture was called) a far superior civilization to that of the Jews and he became impatient with the slow rate of Hellenization of his empire. To move the process along, he outlawed monotheism, persecuted Jews for keeping the Sabbath (the Jewish day of rest and worship), prevented them from performing circumcision and practicing other Jewish customs, and infused the city with Greek symbols. In 168 B.C., Antiochus IV even ordered pagan sacrifices at the holy temple where he had erected an altar to the Greek pagan god Zeus. All of these acts ultimately provoked a Jewish insurrection.

Stripped of their religion and furious over the looting and defiling of their sacred places, the Jews rallied around the **Hasmonean** brothers in what would become known as the **Maccabeean** revolt against the Greeks (named after one of the five brothers, **Judah Maccabee** [the "hammer"]). After winning a series of victories over the Seleucids, the Jews reclaimed Jerusalem, cleansed the Temple and expanded their authority east to the Jordan River, west to the Mediterranean Sea, north to Galilee and south as far as Rafiah.

Jewish sovereignty under the **Hasmonean dynasty** lasted more than 100 years until corruption, greed and brutality under the rule of Judah Maccabee's successors brought the dynasty to an ignoble end. The Romans, who had conquered the Greeks in 146 B.C., officially took over Judah (now called Judea and made part of the province of Syria) in 37 B.C. To govern the area, the Romans appointed King herod who ruled as an absolute monarch with ambitions of leaving a great legacy. Through extensive building projects Herod was respon-

---

[2] The Temple contained riches accumulated from 250 years of tribute collected from the Jews

sible for the construction of aqueducts, palaces, the impressive Masada fortress, theaters, baths, and, most notably, the expansion and embellishment of the **Temple Mount** to an unprecedented splendor.[3]

Rather than endearing his subjects to him by improving the city, the heavy taxation Herod levied to pay for his projects along with his ruthless treatment of dissidents alienated the citizens of Judea. The paranoid king had established an enormous secret police force and was responsible for affixing thousands of suspected conspirators to wooden crosses (an act called crucifixion). In the New Testament of the Bible, it was stated that King Herod ordered the death of every infant boy born in Bethlehem after having heard a prophesy that a rival king of the Jews would be born in that city.

After Herod's death, the rebellious climate and the longing for a Messiah who would come to earth and liberate the Jews continued to grow. It was in this atmosphere that a religiously fanatical group called the **Zealots** was born. In sixty years, the revolutionaries had attracted thousands of small armies who joined them in a four-year insurrection against Roman rule. But they were no match for the disciplined and better-equipped Roman armies. The rebellion was crushed in A.D. 70 by **General Titus** under the Roman Emperor **Vespasian**. Only a small band of rebels held out in Herod's **Masada** fortress for another three years – finally committing mass suicide to avoid being captured by the Romans and being forced to convert. The martyrs earned an esteemed place in Jewish lore.

As punishment for the rebellion, the Romans completely razed the city of Jerusalem, destroyed the Temple and systematically drove Jews out of the city.

Rumors of the Roman Emperor **Hadrian s** plans to build a magnificent Roman city on the ruins of Jerusalem and an altar dedicated to pagan gods on the site of the Temple prompted one last revolt in A.D. 132 led by **Simon Bar Kochba**. The crush of this last revolt by the Romans sealed the fate of the Jews until modern times. After the victory, Hadrian's new pagan city was built as planned and Jews were no longer allowed to visit their holy city. For the next two millennia, Jews were destined to live in foreign land. This exile is known as the "**Diaspora**" (or dispersion).

Adding insult to injury, the Romans renamed Judea the province of **Syria Palestina** (or "**Palestine**") after the Jews' former enemies, the **Philistines**, and called Jerusalem "**Aelia Capitolina**" and dedicated it to the Roman God Jupiter (Zeus to the Greeks).

***

Hanukkah (also Chanukkah)
The "festival of lights" celebrates the Maccabean revolt against the Greeks. According to tradition, when the Jews rededicated the Temple there was only enough oil left to light the *menorah* (a candelabrum that was supposed to burn eternally) for one day. Miraculously, it burned for eight days, long enough to prepare a fresh supply of oil.

---

[3] Today only the Western Wall or "Wailing Wall" of Herod's Temple remains. It is still revered and visited regularly by Jewish worshippers.

JESUS CHRIST

The birth of Jesus of Nazareth had little influence on the world until the faith that bore his name, Christianity, was adopted by the Roman Emperor **Constantine** in the 4th century A.D..

Jesus, born in the time of **King Herod**, (about 4-7 B.C.) was a Jew who shared the same contempt for Roman authority as the rest of the Israelites. Little is known about his childhood except that he was born in Bethlehem[4] and, with his virgin mother, Mary, and father, Joseph (whose lineage could be traced to King David) was taken to Egypt to escape Herod's decree of infanticide. There is little record of his life in the Christian bible (the New Testament) until the age of 30 when he was baptized by **John the Baptist**, perhaps an Essene Jew (a mystical sect of Judaism) who believed in purification and rebirth through ritual cleansing.

In his lifetime, **Jesus** (called **Christ** or "anointed one" by his followers), performed a number of miracles: walking on water, turning water into wine, multiplying fish to feed 5,000 people, healing the sick etc. and preached to his disciples and a host of followers. At that time many of his converts were former sinners or the poor who had been shunned by society, and Jews who saw him as the promised Messiah (the awaited king and deliverer of the Jewish people). As the "Messiah," Jesus prophesied the coming of the "Kingdom of God" as promised in the Torah and instructed Jews to prepare for the event.[5]

But when Jesus began criticizing current religious practices (Jesus railed against the money changers and vendors selling animal sacrifices in the temple, for instance), the Romans saw him as a risk to social order. As the proclaimed "King of the Jews," (by his followers), furthermore, the prophet was also considered a threat to authority. In this age of rebellion, it was not unusual for the Roman leadership to harshly condemn such a dissenter and Jesus Christ was no exception. Roman Procurator, **Pontius Pilate**, sentenced the "Messiah" to an agonizing death by crucifixion.[6]

According to accounts in the New Testament, Jesus rose from the dead three days later. This miraculous Resurrection is celebrated by Christians on Easter Sunday.

Through his disciples, most notably **Paul of Tarsus**, Jesus' message was circulated throughout the Roman Empire attracting pagans (the vast majority of the population who worshiped many gods) and some Jewish converts. Monotheism appealed to many pagans who were drawn to Christianity (as opposed to Judaism) in part because the sole requirement of the new religion was faith. It did not oblige follower to observe the rituals and customs demanded by followers of the Jewish religion (like circumcision, dietary restrictions,

---

[4] It was prophesied in Jewish scripture that the promised Messiah would be born in Bethlehem to a descendant of the House of David.

[5] While the "Kingdom of God" didn't arrive in Jesus' lifetime, Christians believe that the "Second Coming of Christ" is close at hand and will occur once a predetermined course of preparatory events take place.

[6] The act of crucifixion, a Roman form of execution, was forbidden by Jewish law because it was considered torture.

etc.). Poor, hungry and suffering converts also were drawn to the promise of a glorious afterlife in heaven. With only faith as a basis for acceptance, moreover, the religion was accessible to all people, not just those deemed "chosen" by God.

For the next few decades Christians suffered brutal persecution under the Romans (apostles Peter and Paul both died as martyrs in this time) until **Constantine** came to power in the 4th century A.D. According to legend, before going into battle against his rival **Maxentius**, whose army far outnumbered his own, Constantine, a pagan at the time, received a vision from God instructing him to use Christian symbols as a safeguard. With crosses on his soldiers' shields and with the support of Christian troops, Constantine was victorious. Soon after, Constantine declared Christianity the religion of his empire and imposed Christian legislation in his empire -- Sunday became a day of rest, for example, and churches were no longer obligated to pay taxes. Most importantly, he halted the persecution of Christians and helped spread the religion through his endorsement. It was Constantine, moreover, who merged pagan and Christian holidays and decreed that the cross was the official symbol of Christianity.

After Christianity was formally declared the religion of the Empire through the **Nicene Creed** (A.D. 325), Jerusalem enjoyed new prestige as the holiest place in the Christian world. Pilgrims began to make regular trips to the "Holy Land" to visit sites of biblical importance.

In A.D. 331, Constantine transferred the Roman Empire's seat of Government from Rome to a town in the eastern portion of the Empire called **Byzantium** and renamed it Constantinople (present-day Istanbul).

In 395, the Roman Empire was divided among Emperor **Theodosius** s sons. The West, Latin portion became the future "Holy Roman Empire" founded by Charlemagne in A.D. 800 and the seat of Roman Catholicism. The East became known as the Byzantine Empire, after the original name of its capital, and maintained the traditional Greek Orthodox Church. Religious and political differences between the two Christian Empires played a part in the Crusades in the 11th century.

***

Christmas
The date of Jesus' birth was never mentioned in the Bible. Before the fourth century, the date December 25th was designated a holiday in honor of Saturn, the Roman pagan god of agriculture, around the time of the winter solstice. Many traditions now associated with Christmas (gift-giving, Christmas trees, holly, yule logs etc.) were once pagan customs. Today Dec. 25 is celebrated as the day Jesus was born in Bethlehem.

Easter
The day of "Eostre" was originally a pagan holiday commemorating the goddess of offspring (whose symbol was the rabbit) and springtime. On this day people used to exchange colored eggs as a symbol of rebirth. After Constantine's Nicene Creed, the first Sunday after the first full moon of the vernal equinox was deemed a day of observance of Jesus' resurrection after his death by crucifixion ("Good Friday").

ISLAM

In A.D. 577, the birth of one man, **Mohammed**, was about to divide the world into two competing faiths. In the West, Christianity continued to prevail. In the East the prophet Mohammed developed a new religion called "Islam" (which means "submission" to God) that would dominate that part of the world until modern times (currently about one and a half billion people or 22% of the world's population practice Islam). Mohammed's religion was based on tenets found in Judaism and Christianity. In fact, Mohammed considered his role to be complementary to the older faiths by claiming to be the last in a long line of prophets that included Abraham, Moses and Jesus among others.

After Mohammed's death in A.D. 632, the faith spread beyond its place of origin in Mecca and Medina (in present-day Saudi Arabia) to the rest of the Arabian Peninsula and beyond. By 638, a Muslim army under Mohammed's third successor or *caliph*, **Umar**, had swept through Jerusalem subordinating all other religions in the area and bringing the Arabic language to all the people in this rapidly expanding empire (which at its height stretched from Spain to Uzbekistan).

The early conquering Muslims did not force conversion on their new subjects and allowed the Jews and Christians (considered *dhimmies* or "People of the Book") to practice their religions freely within the Islamic Empire. As *dhimmies*, however, they were forbidden to bear arms, serve in public office or build churches and synagogues taller than Muslim mosques. Non-Muslims were also required to pay a special tax or *jizya*.

In order to further assert Islam's dominance in Jerusalem and in an attempt to shift focus away from Islam's center in Mecca to the new capital of Damascus (in Syria) established during the Umayyad Dynasty in 661, the conquering Arab forces built their own religious structures on the remains of the Jewish Temple. Although the city of Jerusalem and the Temple Mount were not mentioned by name in Islam's holy book, the Muslims of that time determined that their prophet Mohammed had taken a "night journey" from the nearest mosque (in Mecca) to the "furthest" or *al-aqsa* mosque (interpreted to mean the site of the Temple Mount in Jerusalem). From this point, Mohammed was believed to have ascended to heaven accompanied by the angel Gabriel (see "Islam" in Palestine section).

On the platform that used to house Herod's Temple, the Muslim's built the **Dome of the Rock** over the spot where Mohammed took his first step up to paradise, and the **Al-Aqsa Mosque** to serve as a meeting place for pilgrims. The site became the third most holy destination to pious Muslims after Mecca and Medina.

The area lost its significance, though, under the rule of the **Abbasids** who took control from the Umayyads in the late 8th century and moved the seat of the *caliphate* east to Baghdad (in present-day Iraq).

In the early 10th century, the Abbasids were, themselves, challenged by a group of radical Shi'ites who called themselves **Fatimids** after Mohammed's daughter, Fatima. By 966, the Fatimids had successfully wrested control over Egypt and Palestine and imposed their fundamental beliefs on the population. The Fatimids persecuted non-Muslims (especially Christians) living in their domain, destroyed their holy sites (including the Church of the Holy Sepulcher built on the site where Jesus Christ was believed to have been crucified) and restricted Christian access to the holy city.

In 1071, Turkish Muslim **Seljuks** captured Jerusalem and the rest of Palestine and prohibited Christians from visiting their holy sites altogether.

In the same year, the Seljuks also fought and beat the Byzantines in the **Battle of Manzikert** and positioned themselves dangerously close to the Roman capital city of Byzantium.

The takeover of the Holy City by Muslims was already troubling to the Christian Kingdoms of Europe, but when Byzantine Emperor **Alexius Comnenus** asked the Pope for help in fighting the Seljuk Turks, the stage was set for what would become a violent 200-year crusade to recover the Holy City from the Muslim infidels.

CRUSADES

By 1071, the **Seljuk Turks** had made their way north from Palestine to the city of **Manzikert** in ancient Armenia (now Eastern Turkey) and appeared to be advancing towards the Byzantine capital, Constantinople. Desperate for reinforcements, the eastern Emperor **Alexius Comnenus** appealed to the western Pope for help. **Pope Gregory**, however, was busy fighting his own battle against the secular leader of the western Holy Roman Empire, **Henry IV**. The church and secular leadership had been vying over spiritual authority in the empire since 1050 in what came to be known as the **Investiture Controversy**.

When Alexius again asked for help in 1095, the new Pope, **Urban II**, answered his call. Leading such a campaign, Urban II hoped, would strengthen the church's authority while helping to mend the rift that had split the Roman empire in half in 1054 (the "**Great Schism**" [7]).

A campaign to liberate the Holy City from the Muslim "infidels" was enthusiastically embraced by impoverished Europeans who were in the middle of a spiritual revolution of their own and were eager to demonstrate their religious devotion. Stories about Seljuk atrocities and desecrations of holy places from Christian pilgrims who had returned from the Holy Land further aroused an already restive population who were anxious to fight their "holy war." Potential crusaders were drawn by promises that their sins would be forgiven if they participated in the Christian war and would be rewarded with a prosperous future. It was also believed that Christians who died while battling infidels would be honored as martyrs and immediately ascend to heaven.

Financially, the Levant (the geographical area of eastern Mediterranean, today, Lebanon, Syria and Israel), which was situated strategically between Asia and the West, was a popular commercial center and capitalistic Crusaders intended to cut out the merchant middlemen by occupying the area and engaging in trade themselves.

The Crusaders successfully occupied Jerusalem in 1099 and immediately massacred the city's Jewish and Muslim inhabitants (Crusaders had already slaughtered thousands of Jews along the way, deeming them "Christ-killers"). Mosques (including the Dome of the Rock) and synagogues were turned into churches and the Church of the Holy Sepulcher was refurbished.

The victory stimulated trade from Asia to the West and helped introduce a number of Eastern ideas and oriental products into Europe that would forever alter Western culture. The Christian hold over the Holy Land, however, was only temporary.

The Muslims regained control over Jerusalem in 1187 under **Saladin**, the sultan of Egypt and Syria, and, after another series of crusades, Palestine finally fell into the hands of the Ottomans who would rule the area for the next 1600 years. (see "Ottoman Empire" in Palestine section)

---

[7] Before the Great Schism, the Christian Church was united under one Pope who traditionally lived in the western portion of the empire (the Holy Roman Empire). Although the rites, doctrines and traditions of the eastern and western churches had been diverging for years, the two were not formally separated until the Great Schism of 1045 when the east became the Eastern Orthodox, Byzantine or Uniate Church and the West became Roman Catholic.

A SHORT HISTORY OF ANTI-SEMITISM[8]

Since their exodus from Egypt in the 13th century B.C., the history of the Jews can be portrayed as a perpetual quest to live in peace in an inviting homeland. During most of their existence, Jews were forced to live away from their mother country where they suffered discrimination and persecution under their alien hosts.

In the course of the first **Diaspora** (or "dispersion") in 722 B.C., Jews living in the northern kingdom of Israel were exiled from Israel by the **Assyrians** and became known as the "**Ten Lost Tribes.**"

A century and a half later, a similar fate befell the Israelites living in Judah who were deported to Babylon where they lived in captivity for the next 70 years. Unlike the "Ten Lost Tribes," however, the Jews from Judah remained cohesive by refusing to assimilate to the pagan lifestyle of their Babylonian captors. Although some members of the community stayed in Babylon after **Cyrus the Great** welcomed the Jews back to Judah, most returned to Israel and lived in relative peace under the Persians and then the Greeks.

As ardently as the Jews believed that their religion and lifestyle were far superior to that of the pagans, so did the Greeks believe that Hellenism was the most advanced culture of the time. Clashes between the pagan Greek rulers and their non-compliant monotheistic Jewish subjects were inevitable, especially considering **Alexander the Great** s ambition to completely unite the cultures and religions of his empire into an integrated whole.

At no time was this clash more evident than during the reign of Seleucid Emperor **Antiochus IV** (175-163 B.C.). Impatient with the progress of Hellenism in Jerusalem, Antiochus decided to force Greek culture on the population by wiping out all competing customs and practices. Jews were persecuted for observing their religion and the city was infused with Greek symbols, including an altar to Zeus in Herod's Temple. A Jewish insurrection led by the **Maccabean** brothers interrupted Antiochus's Hellenizing sweep but not for long.

In 63 B.C., the Romans took over where the Greeks left off and were greeted with more revolts -- the last by the **Zealots** ended tragically in A.D. 73 in the **Masada** citadel with the suicide of 1000 Jewish men, women and children who refused to give up their religion.

As a result of the rebellion, the Romans completely razed the city of Jerusalem, destroyed the temple and systematically drove all the Jews out of the city.

Rumors of Emperor **Hadrian** s plans to build a magnificent Roman city on the ruins of Jerusalem and an altar dedicated to pagan gods on the site of the tem-

---

[8] A Semite is a member of a group of Semitic-speaking people including Arabs, Arameans, Babylonians, Carthaginians, Ethiopians, Hebrews and Phoenicians. The term "anti-Semitism" only came to being in the 19th century and later applied to the hatred of Jews.

ple provoked one last revolt in A.D. 132 led by **Simon Bar Kochba**. The suppression of this last revolt sealed the fate of the Jews until modern times. The new city of **Aelia Capitolina** was built as planned by Hadrian and Jews were forbidden to enter the city. For the next two millennia, Jews were destined to live in foreign lands as the seemingly endless Diaspora (or "dispersion") continued.

While Jews in ancient times were resented because of their refusal to worship pagan gods and conform to local culture, after the birth of Jesus and the spread of Christianity anti-Semitism took a different form.

In Jesus' time, those who recognized the prophet as the proclaimed Messiah were considered a sect of Judaism since their faith was based to a large extent on Jewish scriptures. Although Jews and Christians had different practices and ideologies, the **Nazarenes** (as the sect was called at that time) and the Jews were united in their common fight against the Romans. But the alliance broke down when Emperor **Constantine** declared Christianity the official religion of the Roman Empire in the 4th century.

Through a series of laws and regulations drawn first by Constantine and then his successors, Jews were hit with a series of discriminatory restrictions. In the early 4th century A.D., for example, people living in the Roman Empire were forbidden to convert to Judaism, marriages between Jews and Gentiles (non-Jews) were prohibited, and Jews could face capital punishment for teaching the Torah or encouraging conversion. Under Emperors **Theodosius** and **Justinian**, Jews were not allowed to testify against Christians nor gather in public places and in A.D. 543 the emperor tried to force Jews to postpone **Passover** (the Jewish festival that commemorates the exodus of Jews from Egypt) until after Easter. In A.D. 1215 Jews were required to wear special clothing to distinguish them from Christians.

Jews, the Christians reasoned, were rightfully suffering divine punishment for their role in Christ's crucifixion and their refusal to accept Jesus Christ as Lord and Savior. They were also seen as the final roadblock to religious unity in the Roman Empire and, as such, a threat to Christianity.

Under the Muslims, who appeared on the scene in the 7th century, the Jews fared better. Mohammed had incorporated a number of Jewish ideas and practices into his new faith, including encouraging his followers to pray facing towards Jerusalem, following the same dietary restrictions, fasting, alms giving etc. In turn, he expected the Jews to recognize him as their promised Messiah. Although Mohammed abandoned some of the Jewish customs after he was derided in Medina by Jewish elders, the Muslims continued to consider Jews and Christians respected "people of the book." As long as they paid the required taxes and followed certain regulations (symbolic reminders of their inferior status), "people of the book" (or *dhimmis*) were permitted to practice their religions freely in Muslim territory.

Israel in a Nutshell

With the rise of Islam, moreover, the Mediterranean world was split into Christian and Muslim spheres of influence with the Jews acting as the economic bridge between the empires. Since many traditional occupations were closed to Jews and, due to the Diaspora, fellow Jews could be found in all the key international trading posts (especially in Babylon and Alexandria), it was natural that Jews would engage in trade between China, India, the Middle East and the Christian West. In order to protect their assets from pirates, Jews set up international banking systems based on **Talmudic law**.

Jewish success in trading, however, aroused jealousy and resentment among non-Jews which was manifested in the course of the crusades.

When angry mobs of Christian "holy warriors" set out on their first Crusade in A.D. 1096, their primary objective was to liberate Jerusalem from the Muslim infidels. In their religious zeal, though, they also turned against Jews, the "infidels at home," who were accused not only of being Christ-killers but of complicity with the Muslims. Jews who refused to be baptized were massacred during nine "holy wars" that took place in the years 1096-1272.

The penetration of the Middle East by the Christians opened up trade routes and introduced a new type of economy that required the services of moneylenders (or "usurers"). The pacifist Jews, saddled with discriminatory taxes and becoming increasingly dependent on wealth for their survival (to buy protection from Crusading mobs, for instance), welcomed the opportunity to advance themselves in this occupation. Since the church had banned usury and Judaism didn't forbid lending money and collecting interest from Christians, the Jews had little competition. Emperors and even churches borrowed from the Jews to help pay for construction of palaces and other projects -- often earning Jews important posts in the courts. But it was their practice of collecting interest from poor debtors, who had borrowed money in times of crisis, which was responsible for earning Jewish usurers their bad name. Resentment against Jewish creditors underscored many of the **pogroms** (massacres) that would take place throughout history.

The alien dress, customs and diets of Jews living in foreign lands also mystified and scared the superstitious locals who often turned them into scapegoats for the problems of the day. Jews were accused of ritually killing Christians (as a supposed expression of their "hatred" for Christ) to use their blood in ceremonies (called "**blood libels**"). They were also accused of poisoning wells in order to spread diseases within Christian communities and were even held responsible for the **Black Death** (the bubonic plague) – an accusation that resulted in Jews being hanged or burned alive by angry mobs.

At different times, almost all the countries of Europe had expelled Jews for religious, superstitious and/or economic reasons. In many cases, debts owed to Jews were automatically forgiven once the "usurers" had been driven from England (1290), France (1306 and 1394), Austria (1420) and Spain (1492).

Sephardic Jews

Under the Muslims, a large, influential and flourishing Jewish community had developed for centuries in al-Andalus on the Iberian Peninsula. Jewish tradition in these communities melded with Islamic practices creating a unique form of Judaism practiced by the Spanish Jews (or "Sephardim"). Arabic as well as Hebrew was used for prayers in this community and the Sephardim spoke its own Judeo-Spanish language called **Ladino**.

The 400-year Golden Age of Judaism in Spain ended when the Christians conquered Toledo in 1098 and the rest of Spain by the mid-13th century. In order to homogenize the population under a single faith, the Christians conducted mass conversions of Jews and Muslims. The Jewish converts or **Marranos**, were later accused of practicing Judaism in secret and raising their children according to Jewish custom. Marranos (or "new Christians") were tortured or killed during the 15th century **Spanish Inquisition** and, in 1492, **King Ferdinand** and **Queen Isabella** expelled all Jews who refused to convert to Christianity. Sephardic Jews, once seen as the elite among Jews, resettled in Muslim countries in the Ottoman Empire or joined fellow Jews in other parts of Europe.

Ashkenazic Jews

In the late Middle Ages, the expansion of trade and commerce in Europe (especially in Northern Italy) offered new opportunities for Jewish bankers and money-lenders while the Renaissance (or rebirth) of ideas (through the scientific discoveries of Copernicus, Galileo, Newton etc.) revolutionized man's understanding of the world.

At the same time, the Christian Church was challenged by reformers who protested against corruption and abuses of power by the church leaders. The "**Protestant Reformation**" led by **Martin Luther** (1483-1546) and **John Calvin** (1509-1564) provoked a counter-reformation by the Catholic Church which called for the moral reform of the clergy and the strengthening of Church structures. In the religious fervor, both the Protestant and Catholic churches became eager to stamp out heresy of every kind and the Jews became targets once again. Jewish texts were censored and by the mid-16th century, Jews were segregated into ghettos.

Many of the Jews who had fled the Crusaders and the Spanish Inquisitors and were escaping anti-Semitism in Western Europe, found a haven in Poland and other parts of Eastern Europe (Jews from Europe were called **Ashkenazim** from the Hebrew word for German). Poland, a less-developed frontier land, welcomed the Jews for their skills as merchants, craftsmen and financiers. In time, Poland, whose borders in the 16th century stretched from the Baltic to the Black Sea and included present-day Latvia, Lithuania, Belarus and Ukraine, became home to the largest concentration of Jews in Europe and an important hub for Jewish culture.

Pale of Settlement

After Poland was partitioned in 1795,[9] Russia incorporated the eastern portion of the country and with it, most of the country's Jews. At least half of world Jewry lived in the pan-Slavic, Eastern Orthodox nation. For centuries Jews had been excluded from most areas of Russian life and now, with the incorporation of more than one million Jews, Russian merchants became concerned about Jewish competition. In answer to popular concerns, **Catherine II**, Empress of Russia set out to solve the "Jewish problem" by creating a **"Pale of Settlement"** which would confine Jewish activity to an area of land that roughly corresponded to the districts (made up of Jewish villages or *shtetls*) already heavily occupied by Jews. Except on rare occasions, Jews were prohibited from traveling or living in cities outside the Pale and suffered restrictions, hardships and special taxation within the settlement.

Every Russian tsar who reigned after Catherine II had his own "solution" for dealing with the large Jewish population living within Russia's borders: from attempting to force the Jews to assimilate into Russian society and conscripting Jewish boys into the military (**Nicholas I** decreed that Jewish recruits as young as twelve must serve in the army for a period no less than 25 years), to unofficially sanctioned *pogroms.*[10]

The first of these pogroms was staged after **Tsar Alexander II** had slowly begun to allow Jews to slowly settle in Moscow, St. Petersburg and other prominent Russian cities. As soon as the Jews began to excel in mainstream commerce, though, nationalistic Russians became resentful and accused the "outsiders" of aiming to take over the empire.

Hatred of the Jews soared after Alexander II was assassinated and his anti-Semitic son, **Alexander III**, took the throne. Blamed for the Tsar's murder and of attempting to create a "state within a state" the Jews became targets of more than 200 deadly pogroms throughout Russia in 1881. **"Temporary Laws"** enacted in 1882 (and lasting until 1914) forced Jews to return to a now-reduced Pale of Settlement and to obey a number of discriminatory regulations.

Conditions also deteriorated after the discovery of the so-called **"Protocols of the Elders of Zion,**[11]**"** a forged document allegedly penned by hard-line Zionists outlining a Jewish plot to dominate the world by stirring social unrest and spreading liberal ideas. And the **Russo-Japanese war** of 1905 ushered in some of the worst pogroms Russia had seen resulting in thousands of Jewish deaths and countless more homeless.[12]

---

[9] By 1795, Poland no longer existed as a country; its territory was divided among Austria, Prussia and Russia.

[10] A pogrom is an organized persecution of a minority group, especially of Jews.

[11] The name "Zion" first referred to the Temple Mount under Israel's second king, David. The name was later applied to the city of Jerusalem and then the whole of Israel.

[12] The pogroms of 1905 were inspired in part by the **"Black Hundreds"** a group whose agenda emphasized the annihilation of all Jews.

Dreyfus Affair

West European Jews, meanwhile, had been enjoying much better conditions in an atmosphere of tolerance and liberalism following the French Revolution and the consequent **Declaration of the Rights of Man** (1789). The Capitalist revolution enjoyed in the West opened new doors for Jewish bankers, moneylenders and international traders and brought great wealth to very influential families (most notably the **Rothschilds**). Jews were even permitted to participate in politics and serve in high posts in the military.

In such a progressive atmosphere, therefore, it was particularly disturbing to see a Jewish officer convicted for a crime he didn't commit.

In 1884, a Jewish French Captain by the name of **Alfred Dreyfus** was accused of selling military secrets to the Germans and sentenced to life in prison. Although new evidence later proved that Dreyfus was innocent, the case generated widespread debate and split the country into separate camps of *Dreyfusards* (including **Emile Zola**) who defended the officer and *anti-Dreyfusards*, who maintained his guilt, even after another man was convicted. The affair exposed simmering anti-Semitic sentiments in Europe in the 19th century and stirred up a new group of Jews, the **Zionists**, who began to see an urgent need for a Jewish homeland.

ZIONISM

For thousands of years the Jews anticipated the day when a Messiah, sent by God, would lead them back to Israel. When the time came, said the prophets Isaiah, Jeremiah, Hosea and others, the Temple would be restored, Jerusalem would be established as the center of a world government and Jewish law would become the law of the land.

To Orthodox Jews, the divine event would take place when God willed it and only after certain vital preconditions had been met. Eager religious Zionists, however, believed it was up to the Jews to prepare for the "End of Days" by building a devout society in the *Promised Land* (Israel).

In the 1840s, **Judah (or Yehuda Hai) Alkalai**, a rabbi from Sarajevo, advocated the formation of a representative assembly of Jewish elders to oversee the establishment of colonies in Israel and recommended the revival of Hebrew as a common language. At that time, Hebrew was reserved for religious use while the Jews in the Diaspora spoke more than 70 different languages.

Zevi (or Zwi) Kalischer, a Polish rabbi, also believed that the redemption of Zion would be stimulated by the actions of the Jewish people and appealed to wealthy Jewish families for help in fulfilling the dream of resettlement.

Abraham Isaac (Rav) Kook further held that the best way for the Jewish people to live pure and authentic lives in accordance with Jewish law (one of the prerequisites for the deliverance of a Messiah), would be through the spiritual force created by a unified Jewish homeland. Such a homeland, wrote **Asher Ginsburg (Ahad Ha-am)**, would also give the Jews a renewed sense of national identity -- which had been absent for 2000 years – while acting as a spiritual and cultural center of Jewish life.

Secular Zionists saw Israel as a practical haven for Jewish victims of anti-Semitism. **Moses Hess**, a German Jew, felt that anti-Semitism was deeply and permanently ingrained in the Western psyche. The only way Jews could escape persecution in the Diaspora, where they were perpetually seen as outsiders, would be by creating a Jewish state and embracing a national Jewish character.

Leon Pinsker, like many of his contemporaries who lived during the Enlightenment, at first thought that Jews would eventually be accepted in modern society if they assimilated into their foreign environments. After the wave of pogroms in Russia, though, he, too, came to believe that hatred of the Jews would never disappear and sought a more radical solution to endemic anti-Semitism.

By far the most influential Zionist of the 19th century was **Theodore Herzl**, the son of a rich merchant from Hungary. Like Pinsker, Herzl initially believed Jews could avoid discrimination by assimilating into European culture. After the notorious Dreyfus affair, though, he too was certain that Jews could only be secure in a sovereign Jewish nation. In a 65-page proposal to the Rothschilds, published as *Judenstaat* or "Jewish State," Herzl outlined his plan for the creation of a Jewish commonwealth. With the help of philanthropists and the support of other nations, he reasoned, Jews could settle in a neutral land (preferably in Palestine) and build an infrastructure that would eventually support a gradual stream of Jewish immigrants.

In 1897, more than 200 people from 17 countries gathered in Basel, Switzerland to attend the first Zionist Congress and named Herzl its first president. At the meeting, the **World Zionist Organization** (WZO) stated as its aim: the establishment of a publicly recognized, legally secured home for the Jewish people in *Eretz-Israel.*

In order to legally execute the Zionists' goals, Herzl met with the Sultan of the Turkish Ottoman Empire, which had dominion over Palestine at the time, and Turkey's ally, German Kaiser **Wilhelm II**, to get permission to form a chartered company for the Jews in Palestine.[13] But the cautious Sultan rejected the proposal fearing that establishment of such a company would lead to widespread settlement in Palestine. The setback was all the more disappointing in light of accelerated pogroms in Russia and Romania.

Desperate to find a refuge for Jews fleeing Eastern Europe, Herzl began to consider an offer of land from Britain for the immediate but temporary settlement of Jews in East Africa (commonly known as the **Uganda Project**). The plan was met by bitter opposition by delegates in the Sixth Zionist Congress in 1903, and was finally rejected after Herzl's death in 1905.

While Herzl was trying to secure international recognition for a future Jewish homeland, other organizations, such as **BILU**[14] and "Hovevie Zion" ("Lovers of Zion"), labeled "practical Zionists", were actively establishing communities in Palestine. Through these groups, more than 20,000 Jews (most escaping persecution during Russian pogroms) joined a small group of pioneers living in Palestine in the first of several *aliyahs* [15] (or waves of immigration) that lasted from 1882-1903. A second *aliyah* from 1904 to the start of World War I brought another 40,000 new immigrants from Eastern Europe into Palestine. This group founded **Tel Aviv**, the first modern Jewish city built on land purchased from Ottoman Turks. Until then, most Jews had settled in agricultural colonies (the first established in 1878 called **Petah Tikva**) that were the precursors to agricultural communal settlements called *Kibbutzim*. By the start of World War I in 1914, nearly 100,000 Jews lived in Palestine.

---

[13] In 1900 the Sultan issued a proclamation prohibiting the permanent settlement of Jews in Palestine.

[14] BILU is an acronym for a verse in Isaiah "Beit Ya'akov Lekhu Ve-nelkhal," or "Let us go to the House of Jacob."

[15] "Aliyah" literally means "rise" or "ascent." Jews who made "aliyah" were thought to have risen to a more exalted state.

BALFOUR DECLARATION

Chaim Weizmann, a Russian-Jewish biochemist, was instrumental in bringing the cause of Zionism to the attention of the British.

Weizmann, who moved to England in 1904 to begin a career as a research chemist, had won acclaim and recognition during World War I for his development of a new method of manufacturing acetone (a vital ingredient in explosives and therefore, a great contribution to the war effort). Through his contacts in British society, among them British Foreign Secretary **Lord Balfour** and Lord of the Admiralty **Winston Churchill**, Weizmann was able to persuade the British to support the creation of an independent Jewish state in Palestine.

Britain's sponsorship was outlined in a letter from Balfour to **Lord Rothschild** (a leading British Zionist) on November 2, 1917.

I have much pleasure in conveying to you, on behalf of His Majesty's Government, the following declaration of sympathy with Jewish Zionist aspirations which has been submitted to, and approved by, the Cabinet.

> *His Majesty's Government view with favour the establishment in Palestine of a national home for the Jewish people, and will use their best endeavours to facilitate the achievement of this object, it being clearly understood that nothing shall be done which may prejudice the civil and religious rights of existing non-Jewish communities in Palestine, or the rights and political status enjoyed by Jews in any other country.*

With this declaration, the British hoped to win support of world Jewry during World War I and, more importantly, to persuade the Jews in the U.S. to put pressure on their government to enter the war on Britain's side, and the Jews of Russia[16] to keep Russia in the war. A Jewish nation under British sovereignty in close proximity to the **Suez Canal,** moreover, would help ensure freedom of access through the Canal, the main passageway to the sea route to India and East Africa.

With the support of a major world power and international recognition through the Balfour Declaration the Zionists dream for a Jewish homeland in Palestine was close to becoming a reality.

---

[16] Specifically Jewish Bolsheviks who participated in the 1917 Bolshevik Revolution.

WORLD WAR ONE AND THE BRITISH MANDATE

In December 1917, three years after the Ottoman Turks had joined Germany, Austria-Hungary and Bulgaria (the Central Powers) in war against the Allied forces (which included Britain, France and Russia), British forces led by **Sir Edmund Allenby** marched victoriously into Jerusalem. Once the Central Powers had been defeated the spoils of war were divvied up among the victors.

With the Ottoman Empire defeated, the last obstacle blocking the creation of a Jewish Homeland in Palestine seemed to have been overcome. Representing the Zionists, **Chaim Weizmann** addressed the Allied Powers at the February 1919 **Paris Peace Conference** in order to secure a favorable arrangement for the Jews in Palestine.

A year later, the Allies under the **League of Nations** granted Britain *mandatory* power (or administrative authority)[17] over Palestine to be exercised in accordance with the promises made in the **Balfour Agreement** of November 1917.

Under the terms of the Mandate formalized in **San Remo** on April 24, 1922, the British were responsible for establishing in Palestine a "national home for the Jewish people" with the understanding that "nothing shall be done which might prejudice the civil and religious rights of existing non-Jewish communities in Palestine." The allied powers also recognized the "historical connexion [sic] of the Jewish people with Palestine" and the "grounds for reconstituting their national home in that country."

At the head of the new British administration in Palestine stood **Herbert Samuel**, an English Jew and the first of seven High Commissioners. Although he was a Zionist, Samuel believed that Jews and Arabs could live together in harmony in Palestine and he was committed to keeping order between the groups. While supporting the Zionist community by making it easier for Jews to immigrate and acquire land (which triggered another *aliyah* [wave of immigration] and subsequent Arab riots) he was also mindful of Muslim fears over Zionist ambitions and careful to maintain as much parity between the groups

---

[17] Under a Mandate, territories are governed by more developed nations until the territories are ready to support themselves politically, financially and militarily.

as possible.

To look after Arab affairs, Samuel appointed **Haj Amin al-Husseini** as *Mufti* (chief interpreter of Muslim religious law) of Jerusalem in 1920, and appointed him president of the newly established **Supreme (or Higher) Muslim Council** in 1922.

The **World Zionist Organization** (WZO) set up a Jewish Agency to represent the *yishuv* (Jewish community in Palestine) and facilitate Jewish settlement. In 1920, **David Ben-Gurion** (a politically active Polish Zionist who had moved to Palestine in 1906) led the **Histadrut**, a labor organization that provided social services to the Jews. Many of the institutions created by the Histadrut would dominate Israeli society for decades to come.

Despite Britain's attempt to accommodate the Arab inhabitants, though, the development of Jewish institutions and the influx of Jews into the Arab land of Palestine was resented by the native population who expressed their discontent through increasingly violent riots and demonstrations. When it became apparent that Jews could not rely on the British to protect them after Arab demonstrators attacked the Jewish quarter of Jerusalem in 1920,[18] an underground defense force called the **Haganah** was created. The need for armed forces was all the more evident after Arab riots in 1921 left nearly 50 Jews dead.

As a result of the uprisings, Samuel temporarily suspended immigration (which angered Jews) and set up the **Haycraft Commission of Inquiry** to investigate the causes of the discontent. The conclusions of the Haycraft Commission were published in the **Churchill White Paper**[19] of 1922. While the British government confirmed that the Jews had every right to immigrate and live in a national Jewish home in Palestine, it cautioned that the immigration should not exceed the "economic capacity of the country" nor "be a burden upon the people of Palestine as a whole."

The cycle of violence and appeasement was thus set for the duration of the British occupation. Arab rioting was met with increasing Jewish resolve to protect the *yishuv* and subsequent attempts by the British to accommodate the Arab rioters by limiting Jewish immigration.

In 1929 a confrontation over Jewish access to the **Wailing Wall** (the only remaining portion of Herod's Temple and Judaism's most holy site), turned into another violent attack against Jews by the Arabs and was followed, once again, by an increase in the Zionists' militant resolve.

After the 1929 riots, **Vladimir Jabotinsky**, a Russia "revisionist" Zionist who believed that Palestine would become a Jewish state only when it had a Jewish majority, won many supporters for his proposal that a strong Jewish military force was required to defend the *yishuv* from the Arabs. Only such a force, he

---

[18] Herbert Samuels pardoned the ringleaders of the riots in an attempt to mollify the Arab majority.

[19] A white paper is a section of a written document that states an organization or nation's position on social or political subjects.

reasoned, could compel the Arabs to accept the Zionist objective of creating a Jewish Homeland.

Out of Haganah's inability to defend Jewish civilians in 1929 and Jabotinsky's rhetoric grew a number of militant Jewish Organizations. In 1931, a group of Haganah members left the organization to join **Betar**, a Zionist movement founded in Latvia that rejected the Haganah and Histadrut's policy of self-restraint. In 1937, more Haganah members joined Betar and formed another militant underground organization called **Irgun**. In 1939, the **Stern Gang** (also known as **Lehi**) split from Irgun to form an even more extreme terrorist group.

At the same time, British sympathies were increasingly turning toward the Arabs. The pro-Zionists who had helped create the Jewish state (Balfour, Churchill and Samuels) had been replaced in the British government by a less sympathetic party under Prime Minister **Ramsay MacDonald** and a new Colonial Secretary by the name of **Lord Passfield**.

Under the new regime, Jewish immigration policies and Jewish land purchases were examined and the creation of a legislative council with a numerically representative committee was considered. In 1929, MacDonald proposed a governing body with ten Muslims, three Jews and two Christians.

In the white paper published by Lord Passfield in October 1930, the British government argued that there wasn't enough arable land in Palestine to support both the incoming Jews and the Arabs and suggested that immigration be curtailed or even terminated. The white paper was met with sharp criticism by Jews worldwide who had an even greater reason to guard their rights to immigrate - - in Germany, a frightening development was taking place that was about to change the fate of millions of Jews.

Adolf Hitler

Faced with a severe economic crisis and suffering from international dishonor after World War I, German citizens were looking for a savior. In response, German politicians adopted extreme nationalistic platforms to win supporters. At the forefront was the Nazi Party of **Adolf Hitler**.

Hitler's rise to power in the 1930s sent waves of Jewish immigrants to Palestine. As the design of the Fuhrer ("leader") became clearer, the flow increased. In 1933, German Jews were excluded from most civil servant jobs and the media. After the Nuremberg decrees of 1935, Jews were no longer considered citizens of the Reich[20] and by the end of the decade, Jews were excluded from using railroad sleeper cars and other public institutions, their economic activity was severely restricted and they were required to carry special identity cards.

Every intensification of discrimination in Germany was matched by corresponding leaps in immigration numbers to Palestine – many times in excess of the limits set forth in the **Passfield Paper**. In less than a decade, the number of

---

[20] Germany was called the 3rd Reich under the Nazis.

Jews rose from 17% to about 31% of the population in Palestine and Arab hostility grew proportionately.

Between 1936 and 1939, Arab attacks against Jewish immigrants inspired Jews to adopt more militant methods of defense and pushed the British (who were preparing for another World War) to apply stricter measures to maintain order.

Peel Partition Plan

In July 1937, a report issued by a British investigative committee headed by **Lord Robert Peel** (called the **Peel Commission**) concluded that Arabs and Jews could not resolve their problems and suggested a partition of the land into three parts. The Jews would be assigned a strip of land in the northwest along the coast of the Mediterranean Sea, while Jerusalem, with a corridor to the ocean, would remain in British hands. The remainder would belong to the Arabs.

The Partition Plan was partially accepted by the Zionists. Although some Zionists, Jabotinsky among them, believed the area was inadequate for a Jewish homeland, others, like Ben-Gurion, believed the establishment of a Jewish state, however small, would be a positive first step towards full realization of a homeland in Palestine.

The Arabs, on the other hand, completely rejected the Plan and violently expressed their opposition. A full-scale Arab revolt was severely repressed by the British government in 1938 and the Peel Partition Plan was abandoned.

Again the British attempted to appease the Arabs by punishing the Jews. The British white paper published in 1939 (the "**MacDonald White Paper**") ruled out the creation of a Jewish state and decreed that only 75,000 Jews would be allowed to settle in Palestine within a five-year period. After that time, Jewish immigration would be prohibited altogether unless the Palestinian Arabs approved. The Balfour Declaration had been effectively dismissed at a time when Jews most desperately needed a haven.

WORLD WAR II

Close to ten million Jews lived in Europe in 1939 when the **MacDonald White Paper** ruled that no more than 75,000 Jews would be allowed to immigrate to Palestine within a 5-year period. That same year, **Hitler** s army swept through the continent in a lightning war (*blitzkrieg*) that quickly engulfed Poland and later, Western Russia, which then meant a large number of Jews were incorporated into Nazi Germany. But as the Jews of Europe were suffering internment in ghettoes, savage persecution and eventual mass-slaughter, the British stubbornly maintained the immigration quotas stated in the white paper allowing only 1,500 Jews to enter Palestine per month.

After Allied victory was declared on May 8, 1945, millions of Jewish survivors, many liberated from Nazi concentration camps, were stranded in Europe. Their homes had been destroyed or occupied, immigration quotas set up in the U.S., Britain and other countries limited international migration and the pall of death and hatred of Jews was still thick in Poland and Germany.

The massacre of six million Jews had also severely affected the Jewish psyche. Jews realized that assimilation into foreign cultures would not guarantee Jewish safety and passive acceptance of anti-Semitism could lead to dangerous consequences. The ambitions of the Zionists, therefore, took on a dramatically new appeal.

To get around British restrictions, Zionist groups after the war set-up organizations to help smuggle Jews illegally into Palestine (called the *Aliyah Bet* or "illegal immigration"). Often sailing aboard dilapidated ships, some of the Jewish passengers successfully penetrated British blockades set up along the coast of Palestine. Most did not. The ships that were intercepted by the British were redirected to Cyprus where "displaced person" (DP) camps had been set up to house the illegal immigrants until their status was decided.

The story of one of those ships, the **Exodus**, became the subject of a novel by **Leon Uris** and a popular film by the same name starring Paul Newman. The Exodus set off from France to Palestine in July 1947 with more than 4,000 Jewish refugees aboard. Before it reached Gaza, though, it was intercepted by the British navy and the passengers were deported -- not to Cyprus, as was the usual policy, but back to Europe. When the Jews refused to disembark in France, the ship was redirected to Hamburg, Germany where the passengers were forcibly dragged from the ships in front of news cameras and interred in DP camps. The incident received international attention and turned public opinion against the British.

In Palestine, meanwhile, Jewish militancy was mounting uncontrollably. Members of the **Stern Gang** began firing on police and soldiers, burned oil

---

[21] Part of the reason Britain tried to appease the Arabs at the expense of the Jews was to protect Britain's Middle East oil interests.

refineries,[21] interrupted transportation and threatened British army installations. The Irgun, under its new head **Menachim Begin**, also terrorized British soldiers, released prisoners from the impenetrable Acre Prison and bombed the **King David Hotel**, where the British had set up their military and civil administrative headquarters.

By February 1947, the British had grown weary of the Palestinian situation and turned to the United Nations for help.

The eleven-member body set up to investigate the situation, the **UN Special Committee on Palestine** or **UNSCOP**, recommended an end to the British Mandate and the partition of Palestine into Arab and Jewish states. It also suggested putting Jerusalem, the site of Jewish, Muslim and Christian holy places, under international control. The plan, which was similar to the Peel Partition Plan, granted the Jews 55% of Palestine including the northeastern strip and the Negev Desert.

The arrangement was greeted positively by most of the Jews (though some, like Begin and the Irgun members, continued to believe that *Eretz-Israel*

UN Partition Plan 1947

Jewish State
Arab State
UN Administration

Beirut
LEBANON
Damascus
SYRIA
Haifa
Jaffa
Jerusalem
Amman
Gaza
TRANSJORDAN
EGYPT
Sinai Peninsula
Aqaba
Red Sea
Gulf of Aqaba
SAUDI ARABIA
St. of Tiran

rightfully belonged to the Jewish people in its entirety) and the British agreed to leave the country by August 1948.

The Arabs, however, aggressively rejected the decision and deemed the Jews "imperialistic invaders." Violence broke out immediately after the U.N. announced the partition on November 29, 1947 prompting the British to leave four months early.

In the midst of rioting on May 14, 1948, Ben-Gurion and other Israeli leaders signed Israel's **Declaration of Independence**.

1948 WAR OF INDEPENDENCE

Just hours after **David Ben-Gurion** declared Israel an independent state on May 14, 1948, the new state's Arab neighbors declared war. Egypt, Syria, Transjordan (the predecessor to Jordan), Lebanon and Iraq tested the fledgling nation's might by invading Israel from all sides. But the largely ill-trained, and inexperienced Arab troops were no match for the combined forces of the **Haganah** (Israel's de facto army), the **Irgun**, **Stern Gang** and more than 20,000 Jewish World War II veterans who fought for Israel's survival. Although numerically inferior, the Israeli forces were better organized, better equipped and better prepared to repel the military assault of the Arab forces.

By February 1949, Egypt was forced to negotiate an armistice agreement with Israel followed by Lebanon in March, Transjordan in April and Syria in July (Iraq withdrew its forces without signing an agreement.)

As a result of the war, Israel expanded its territory beyond the borders laid out in the U.N. Partition Plan but lost Samaria and Judea (to be called the **West Bank** from that point on) and the Old City of Jerusalem[22] (the site of the Wailing Wall and the Al-Aqsa Mosque) to Transjordan.

Nearly 1% of the Palestinian Jewish population had died in the War of Independence and many Jewish villages and synagogues had been destroyed. Moreover, Israel was now surrounded by hostile Arab states that were bitterly opposed to the creation of a Jewish homeland and it was faced with a total economic embargo imposed by the **Arab League**. All products manufactured by Israelis were boycotted by all Arab states as were goods sold by companies that did business with the Jewish state. All border crossings in and out of Israel were closed and all planes flying to or from Israel were forbidden from entering Arab air space.

Even in the midst of such economic and political hostility, though, Israel managed to create a functional, U.N.-recognized[23] Jewish state. **David Ben-Gurion**, former chairman of both the **World Zionist Organization** and the Jewish Agency, was elected Prime Minister and **Chaim Weizmann** became the state's first President (a ceremonial position). A constituent assembly was created in October 1948 (which would become the state's first legislative branch called the **Knesset**) and plans were made to draw up a formal constitution.[24]

---

[22] Israel took control of the urban western part of Jerusalem -- the "New City."

[23] Israel was admitted to the U.N. in May 1949.

[24] The proposed constitution was never ratified because of disagreements between orthodox Jews -- who believed the Torah should serve as Israel's constitution -- and secular Zionists.

Israel in a Nutshell

Questions regarding the theocratic or democratic nature of Israel's government and the need for a secular constitution as opposed to the use of the Torah as the nation's legislative manual would continue to vex the nation's administrators for decades. But the country's basic laws guaranteeing religious and civil rights for all Israeli citizens were embraced by all.

Socialism

From the early agricultural cooperatives established in the 19th century to Ben-Gurion's Histadrut Labor Union (which controlled nearly all means of production) the state of Israel was destined to adopt a socialist infrastructure with state-owned institutions, utility companies, airline and state-sponsored social welfare and health benefits. The small nation's reliance on foreign capital from wealthy capitalist countries (namely the US and Western Europe), however, prevented Israel from setting up a completely socialist state.

Law of Return and Immigration

One of the first legislative changes initiated by the new Israeli leaders was the country's policy on immigration. In 1950, the Knesset passed the **Law of Return** which granted every Jewish person in the world the right to become an Israeli citizen. The announcement predictably led to a tremendous influx of Jews. Hundreds of thousands of people flooded into Israel, nearly doubling the existing Jewish population by 1951 and drawing on the nation's already limited resources. The emerging state hadn't yet built a national economy and was not prepared to accommodate the flood of newcomers. Those who had come from poorer nations or had no resources of their own, therefore, had to live in transit camps until they could be incorporated into Israeli society.

Economic and social discrepancies among the immigrant groups also led to social tensions. The wealthier, more established Jews from Europe (mostly Ashkenazim) rebuffed the poorly educated, welfare-dependent Jews who arrived from countries in the former Ottoman Empire (primarily Sephardic Jews escaping discrimination). Sephardic Jews, in turn, resented the political elitism of the Ashkenazic Jews.

Palestinian Refugees

While Israel was trying to manage its own growing population, the Palestinian Arabs were dealing with a different problem. Hundreds of thousands of Palestinians who had fled the country during the war of 1948 -- hoping to return after the Jews had been "annihilated" by the Arab coalition -- were now living in squalid overcrowded refugee camps across the border in Syria, Jordan and Lebanon. Much of the land and property they had abandoned, furthermore, had been appropriated by incoming Jews who were desperate for housing.

Angry and displaced, the landless Palestinian refugees resorted to terror to try to win back their property and, encouraged by their Arab brethren, began to participate in waves of attacks against the Israeli settlers. The raids eventually became more organized and bases of operation sprung up in neighboring countries (Jordan, Lebanon and Egypt) to train and fund the terrorist groups, or *fedayeen*. Between 1951-1956, hundreds of *fedayeen* attacks in Israel left more than 400 Israelis dead and many more injured. Egypt's participation in *feday-*

een activity eventually led to the eruption of the **Sinai Campaign in 1956.**

SINAI CAMPAIGN 1956

Since Israel's declaration of independence in 1948, many changes had taken place in the Middle East. Syria's government was plagued by a series of military coups; Jordan's **King Abdullah** was assassinated in 1951 by a Palestinian extremist who feared that he would make a separate peace with Israel; and Egypt's premier **Mahmoud Fahmy El-Nokrashy** and **King Farouk** were replaced by the young general **Gamal Abdel Nasser.**

Nasser, a pan-Arab nationalist, had taken on the battle against Israel by arming and training the *fedayeen,* who had been making raids into southern Israel from Egyptian-controlled Gaza Strip, and building his nation's arsenal with arms imported from the Soviet Union through Czechoslovakia.

Nasser intensified hostilities by blockading the **Straits of Tiran**, which cut off Israel's supply route to Asia, and nationalizing the **Suez Canal**, a move that also threatened British and French interests.[25]

The British, French and Israelis, therefore, shared a desire to overthrow Nasser and take back the waterways. In a secret agreement, the three nations plotted an attack against Egypt.

In late October the **Israeli Defense Force** (IDF)[26] under the command of **Moshe Dayan** captured the Gaza Strip and the Sinai Peninsula. A few days later, the British and French took over the Suez Canal area.

The allied forces were compelled to withdraw their troops from Egyptian territories, however, after the United States, the Soviet Union and the United Nations expressed strong opposition to the venture. To maintain order, the United Nations stationed Emergency Forces (**UNEF**) on the Egyptian territories of the Gaza Strip and at **Sharm el Sheikh** on the Straits of Tiran.

Although Israel was forced to withdraw its troops from Sinai, the war was seen as a success by Israel's leaders. U.N. peacekeeping forces had been deployed to protect Israeli waterways, the *fedayeen* raids from Gaza stopped and Israel's image as a military power had been enhanced. But the relative peace that followed the Sinai Campaign was tenuous.

---

[25] The Suez Canal was built by a private company owned primarily by British and French shareholders. Access through the canal, which was the only waterway from the Mediterranean Sea to the Red Sea, was vital to European shipping to and from the East.

[26] The IDF was formed during the War of Independence from the combined Israeli forces.

SIX-DAY WAR 1967

The U.N. presence in the Gaza Strip had temporarily put a stop to *fedayeen* attacks in Israel but it didn't solve the mounting problems among Israelis, the Palestinians and the Arab world.

Syria, Israel's neighbor in the northeast, was one of Israel's most belligerent adversaries. In the eyes of the Syrians, not only had Israel claimed a chunk of land from their ancient territory of "Greater Syria" (which once included Jordan, Lebanon, Israel and modern-day Syria) but it also threatened their water supply.

The streams that flowed from the high peaks of the Golan to the Jordan River provided Israel with most of its fresh water supply. In order to bring this water to arid parts of the country the government built a network of pipes and aqueducts. The Syrians, however, planned to build their own irrigation canal system at the river's source that would have dried up the valuable riverbed.

Egypt was aware of the tensions that were mounting between Israel and Syria over the precious water supply and called an Arab summit in 1964 to discuss the issue. The program at the Cairo meeting, though, went far beyond arguments over the Jordan River and included discussion regarding the ultimate destruction of "imperialist" Israel.

Rather than engaging Israel in a war that the Arab states were not prepared to fight, alternative courses of action were suggested and agreed upon, among them: diversion of water from the Jordan River to Syria and Lebanon in the north, the establishment of a united Arab front under Egypt's command and the creation of the **Palestinian Liberation Organization** to take on the cause of the Palestinian people. Soon after, another Palestinian terrorist group called **al-Fatah**, headed by **Yasser Arafat** and aided by Syria's military, began to engage in guerrilla assaults against Israel from the West Bank and across the Lebanese and Syrian borders.

Between 1965 and 1966, Syrian attacks from the mountains of the **Golan Heights** against men, women and children living in Israeli farms and villages below, grew more and more frequent forcing the Israeli military to take action. In April 1967, the Israeli Defense Force shot down six Syrian MiG fighter jets supplied by the Soviet Union, setting off a six-day war that put Israeli-Arab relations into a perilous tailspin.

In retaliation for Israel's aggression towards Syria and acting on a false Soviet report that Israel was concentrating large forces on the border in preparation for war, Egypt, which was bound to Syria by a defense pact made in 1966, told the U.N. Peacekeeping troops (UNEF) to leave the Sinai Desert and deployed its own troops along the Israeli border. On May 22, Egypt closed the Gulf of Aqaba and ordered a blockade of all shipments to and from Israel through the

Straits of Tiran in direct violation of the armistice agreements drawn up in 1956. By the end of May, Jordan, Iraq and Lebanon had joined Egypt and Syria in their hostile rhetoric leaving Israel surrounded and outnumbered by belligerent Arab forces.

Without help from powerful western allies - since Britain and France had reneged on their commitment to guarantee the freedom of Israeli navigation and the U.S. was embroiled in its own war in Vietnam - Israel had decided to unilaterally take defensive measures.

On June 5, 1967, Israelis launched a preemptive strike on Egypt's Air Force while the pilots were eating breakfast. With the Egyptian air force effectively neutralized,[27] the Israelis turned to Jordan where they inflicted the same type of damage on its airfield. For the next five days, Israeli troops fought a heroic ground battle in Sinai and the Golan Heights and recaptured the Old City from Jordan. For the first time in 2000 years the site of the Holy Temple was entirely in Jewish hands.

In less than a week, Israel had taken control of the Sinai Peninsula, the Golan Heights, the Gaza Strip, the West Bank and East Jerusalem -- more than tripling the size of territory under its control before the war and instantly increasing its Arab population by three quarters of a million.

Although by the end of the war Israel's armies were strong enough to march into the Middle East capitals of Cairo, Damascus and Amman, the government instead declared a cease-fire and exulted in its new prestige as a dominant and permanent military power in the region.

Hundreds of thousands of Israelis moved into the newly acquired territories and celebrations took place at the newly liberated Wailing Wall in East Jerusalem.

National pride, though, was shadowed by the deep awareness that the entire Arab world was still hoping for the nation's annihilation and in recognition that the superpowers could not always be relied upon to help the Jewish state in times of crisis. **U.N. Security Council Resolution 242** passed on November 22

---

[27] More than three hundred Egyptian combat planes, nearly the entire fleet, were destroyed within two hours.

Israel in a Nutshell

1967 delineated Israel's insecurity.

According to the Resolution a "just and lasting peace in the Middle East" depended on the "termination of all claims of belligerency and respect for and acknowledgement of the sovereignty, territorial integrity and political independence of every State in the area and their right to live in peace within secure and recognized boundaries free from threats or acts of force." Other guarantees included the "freedom of navigation through international waterways in the area" and the "establishment of demilitarized zones."

United Nations Security Resolution 242

Adopted by the U.N. General Assembly on November 22, 1967 in the aftermath of the Six Day War of 1967.

(Condensed)
The Security Council,

Emphasizing the inadmissibility of the acquisition of territory by war and the need to work for a just and lasting peace, in which every State in the area can live in security,

Emphasizing further that all Member States in their acceptance of the Charter of the United Nations have undertaken a commitment to act in accordance with Article 2 of the Charter

1. Affirms that the fulfillment of Charter principles requires the establishment of a just and lasting peace in the Middle East which should include the application of both the following principles:

    a. Withdrawal of Israeli armed forces from territories occupied in the recent conflict
    b. Termination of all claims or states of belligerency and respect for and acknowledgement of the sovereignty, territorial integrity and political independence of every State in the area and their right to live in peace within secure and recognized boundaries, free from threats or acts of force

2. Affirms further the necessity

    a. For guaranteeing freedom of navigation through international waterways in the area
    b. For achieving a just settlement of the refugee problem
    c. For guaranteeing the territorial inviolability and political independence of every State in the area, through measures including the establishment of demilitarized zones

Controversy:

The ambiguity of Resolution 242, which was never fully implemented, provoked lengthy discussion and disagreement among Arab and Israeli groups. Among the controversial issues:

a. Withdrawal of Israeli armed forces from territories occupied in the recent conflict

Translations of this clause differ over a "missing" article before the word "territories." The French version of the Resolution (French and English languages are both recognized by the United Nations) translates as a requirement that Israeli forces withdraw from "all" occupied territories as opposed to a "partial" withdrawal implied by the English text. Palestinians claim that the preamble, which deems the "acquisition of territory by war inadmissible," implies that Israel illegally acquired territory in the Six-Day War and therefore was obliged to withdraw back to its former borders.

Israelis who have argued against "full withdrawal" claimed that the borders defined in June 1967 were simply armistice lines that were expected to shift as populations in the areas fluctuated. This fluctuation, they reasoned, should be considered in any future trades of "land for peace." This line of reasoning has been embraced by supporters of Israeli settlements in the occupied territories.

b.   respect for and acknowledgement of the sovereignty, territorial integrity and political independence of every State in the area

To the Palestinians, this clause implied recognition of Israel's right to exist which they were not prepared to accept.

c.   and their right to live in peace within secure and recognized boundaries free from threats or acts of force

Ariel Sharon claimed that Israel's dominion over the West Bank, Gaza and East Jerusalem was necessary for security reasons - to ensure that the country's boundaries would be "free from threats or acts of force." He concluded that as long as Palestinian incursions threatened the state, Israel's occupation of the controversial areas should be recognized as the nation's right per Resolution 242.

d. .. a just settlement of the refugee problem

The Palestinians rejected Resolution 242 because this clause did not specifically mention them by name.

YOM KIPPUR WAR (Ramadan War, October War) 1973

The 1967 War ended with Israel's acquisition of the Golan Heights, Sinai, the West Bank and East Jerusalem but it only intensified bad relations between Israel and the Arab states. In the years following the Six-Day War, the Jewish people had to contend with a "war of attrition" by Palestinians and their Arab sponsors (Egypt primarily), that aimed at weakening the country financially and politically and undermining Israeli morale. The Egyptians shelled Israeli military targets near the Suez Canal while Palestinian guerrillas terrorized Jews living inside and outside the country.[28]

Disagreements over the terms of **Resolution 242** also frustrated Nasser's successor **Anwar Sadat**[29] who was eager to bring Sinai back into Egyptian hands. Several times in 1971 and 1972, the Egyptian president threatened to go to war to force Israel to fulfill the terms of the UN Resolution as he interpreted it -- that is, Israel's full withdrawal from territories it occupied in the course of the 1967 war. After a series of empty threats, Sadat finally acted on his belligerent rhetoric in 1973.

On Yom Kippur, Judaism's Day of Atonement that is customarily spent fasting and attending synagogue, Egyptian and Syrian troops jointly attacked Israel on two fronts. In the north, Syrian troops pushed their way through the Golan Heights while Egyptian forces attacked the few Israeli troops stationed along the eastern bank of the Suez Canal. Although Israel's Prime Minister, **Golda Meir**, had been warned of an impending invasion by Jordan, she had decided not to assemble Israel's reserve troops. In the first few days of the Yom Kippur War, therefore, while most of the country's soldiers were observing the holy day in the synagogues, the Israelis were easily defeated.

The tide began to turn once Israel's Defense Force was fully mobilized. The Syrians were driven out of territories they had conquered early on and the Israelis advanced on the Suez Canal area. The reversal of fortune was troubling to the Soviets who swiftly re-supplied the Arab states with armaments

The Soviet involvement in turn provoked the Americans who provided aid to the Israelis. The Arab oil-producing states then imposed oil embargoes against the U.S. to protest America's support for Israel.

By the time a ceasefire was declared, the Syrian offensive had been repelled and Israeli forces under the command of **Ariel Sharon** had broken through Egypt's battle lines and were approaching Cairo. Negotiations between the General Secretary of the Soviet Union, **Leonid Brezhnev**, and American Secretary of

---

[28]On September 5, 1972, 11 Israeli athletes were taken hostage during the Munich Olympics by Palestinian terrorists who were demanding the release of 200 Arab prisoners. The hostages and most of the terrorists were killed in a shootout a few days later.

[29] Gamal Abdul Nasser died from a heart attack on September 28, 1970 and Anwar Sadat became president of Egypt.

Israel in a Nutshell

State **Henry Kissinger**, resulted in the creation of **UN Security Resolution 338** which called for dialogue between the warring parties and the implementation of **Resolution 242**. Israeli and Egyptian military leaders met a few days later to discuss how to disengage their troops.

The war had a terribly demoralizing effect on Israel. Not only had thousands of troops been killed in the course of the battle but the country's national self-confidence and reputation as an invincible force had been deeply damaged.

Much of the blame for Israel's lack of preparedness was placed on Israel's government, forcing Golda Meir and the country's defense minister, **Moshe Dayan** to resign.[30] The dissatisfaction was reflected in Israel's parliament in 1977 when the **Labour Party**, was replaced by the more conservative, right-wing **Likud Party** with **Menachem Begin** as its leader. (See "Israeli Politics")

The war also demonstrated the growing influence of the Arab oil producing states and Israel's increasing reliance on the United States financially and politically. It was America's Secretary of State, **Henry Kissinger**, who orchestrated the truce between the belligerent parties ending the war through his "**shuttle diplomacy**" ("shuttling" between Jerusalem and the Arab capitals) and U.S. president **Jimmy Carter**, who called Egyptian president Anwar Sadat and Israeli Prime Minister Menachem Begin to the bargaining table in 1978 (Sadat refused to deal directly with the Israelis and would only talk through the Americans).

At the peace talks, Sadat claimed to represent the Palestinians and Israel's Arab neighbors when he demanded that Israel withdraw from Gaza and the West Bank and that a Palestinian state be created with its capital in Jerusalem.

Menachim Begin, on the other hand, claimed that Judea, Samaria and the Gaza strip were not occupied states but rather integral parts of *Eretz-Israel* that had been liberated by the Israelis during the Six-Day War. Begin had made it one of his priories to built Jewish settlements on the land that he considered rightly belonging to Israel.

The two parties finally compromised, though, with agreement that Israel would relinquish the Sinai in return for Egypt's recognition of Israel's right to exist -- the first Arab state to do so. Both Sadat and Begin were awarded the Nobel Peace Prize for their cooperation but faced stiff opposition in their own countries over the compromise.

Two years later, Anwar Sadat was assassinated by an Islamic extremist, who criticized the Prime Minister for entering into a bilateral agreement with the enemy to secure Egypt's own interests (the return of Sinai) and ignoring the Palestinian problem in the process.

---

[30] Three years later, in 1977, Moshe Dayan was offered the post of Minister of Foreign Affairs and participated in negotiations with Egypt.

PALESTINIANS

From the rebellion in 1929 until today, Israel has been fighting an ongoing battle with the indigenous population over rights to Israeli land. In the decades leading up to independence, property was readily available to Zionist organizations who purchased blocks of arable land (at premium prices) from absentee Arab landlords to accommodate the growing number of Jewish immigrants. While the land sales benefited the Arab capitalists, they hurt the Palestinian peasants who were left destitute and homeless. Throughout the British Mandate period, these displaced Palestinians blamed their troubles on the immigrants and fought to get their share of the slowly developing country.

In 1948, Palestinians fled from their homes en masse to escape fighting between Arab and Jewish forces. Most settled temporarily in Gaza and the West Bank while others went to neighboring countries to await the expected defeat and ultimate expulsion of the Zionist settlers. But victory didn't come to the Arabs.

In 1967, Palestinian hopes were renewed when Syria joined Egypt in a double-fronted assault on the Israelis. But the battle resulted in another defeat for the Arab forces and the Israelis moved into Gaza, the West Bank and Sinai Peninsula prompting hundreds of thousands of Palestinians to join their compatriots outside the new borders, again, to await the day when they could return.

Middle and upper class Palestinians rented apartments on a short-term basis in nearby Arab cities (Amman, Beirut, Cairo, Damascus) and enjoyed relatively comfortable living conditions in exile. But as "foreigners," in their host countries, they were disenfranchised politically (except in Jordan) and limited economically.

The vast majority of displaced Palestinians, however, settled in refugee camps that were initially supported by the Arab governments and later supplied primarily by the **U.N. Relief and Works Agency** (**UNRWA**). The standard of living in these primitive tent cities was poor with inadequate sewage systems, roads, medical services, schools etc. Conditions worsened as the Palestinian population grew. Young Palestinians (more that 50% of the population by the 1970s were minors) grew restless as they looked toward bleak futures devoid of educational and vocational opportunities. All Palestinians yearned for the liberation of Palestine and many eagerly joined resistance groups to fight for the cause. Collectively, these bitter guerrilla warriors became known as *fedayeen*.

PLO

In 1958, a group of university student activists in the Gaza Strip (**Yasser Arafat** among them) joined together to form **Fatah**, an underground organization dedicated to the Palestinian cause.

About the same time, Arab leaders meeting in Cairo created a representative body called the **Palestine Liberation Organization** (PLO) with **Ahmed al Shukairy** at its head and the **Palestinian Liberation Army** as its military wing.

After the Arab defeat in the Six-Day War in 1967 and due to Shukairy's incompetent leadership, the PLO (essentially a pan-Arab creation) was discredited in the eyes of most Palestinians. Its only hope for survival was to change its leadership to give it a more Palestinian character. Yasser Arafat, then the head of the popular Fatah group, was Shukairy's logical successor and in February 1969, he was elected Chairman of the Executive Committee of the PLO.

Within two decades, the Palestinian Resistance Movement had become structured and was actively working with recruits in the refugee camps. With the help of the PLO and other resistance groups, refugee tents were replaced by cinder-block houses with running water, welfare institutions were established and police and paramilitary squads were trained and organized. The former tent cities began to resemble independent states that directly challenged the authority of the governments of their host countries.

Black September
In addition to unwelcomed Palestinian autonomy in Jordan, where the bulk of Palestinians had set up residence, the country's King **Hussein** became increasingly disturbed by Palestinian militant activity against Israel staged from within its borders.[31] Animosity between the Palestinians and the Jordanians came to a head in September 1970 (called "Black September" by the Palestinians) when King Hussein launched a brutal offensive against Palestinian militant groups. After a year of bloody fighting the PLO and other Resistance groups were forced to move their operations to Lebanon.

Lebanon
While in Lebanon, which had become weak after years of civil war (1975-1982), the PLO and other organizations flourished until they eventually controlled Lebanon's southern Israeli boundary. From their new stronghold Palestinian militants were able to conduct regular small-scale assaults against Israeli civilians on the other side of the border. That all changed, though, after war hawk **Ariel Sharon** was made Israel's Defense Minister in 1981.

---

[31] In the late 1960s, for example, the PFLP, a militant organization that acted separately from the PLO, had conducted a number of hijacking attacks on Israeli planes forcing them to land in Jordan.

LEBANON WAR 1982

Since Lebanon's independence in 1941 the country maintained a delicate balance between its Christian citizens (most of them Maronite Christians) and Muslims. With each wave of Palestinian immigrants from Israel, though, the balance was disturbed. The refugees also extended the Israeli-Arabic crisis to Lebanon's southern border by staging raids against the Jewish nation from bases established in Lebanon. These incursions, in turn, provoked retaliatory strikes by the **Israeli Defense Force.**

Although the Lebanese government attempted to curb the fighting by trying to curtail Palestinian guerrilla activity through military action, they were not able to stop the cycle of violence.

In 1975, a few years after the PLO had transferred its headquarters to Lebanon following their expulsion from Jordan, the social balance in the country collapsed. Hostility between the ruling Lebanese Christians (who wanted to maintain their power) and the Lebanese Muslims and others who wanted changes in the Lebanese government, thrust the country into a destructive civil war that lasted for decades.

In the midst of the chaos, the PLO set up command centers in Beirut and southern Lebanon and launched repeated attacks on Israeli targets across the border. As before, these attacks were followed by armed reprisals. An event in 1978, however, compelled Israelis to step up their attacks.

In March of that year a group of Fatah guerrillas who had infiltrated Israel by sea, hijacked a bus on a coastal highway just north of Tel Aviv. As the hijackers navigated the bus south to the city, a gun battle ensued that left 32 Israelis dead and 82 wounded -- most of the casualties had been civilians. When it was determined that the guerrillas had come from Lebanese bases, the Israelis prepared for a full-fledged assault.

Days after the hijacking, 20,000 Israeli troops invaded Lebanon,(called **"Operation Litani"**), cleared the Lebanese border of *fedayeen* and created a buffer zone before they were commanded by the United Nations and the U.S. to withdraw their troops. To monitor the retreat and restore international peace, the United Nations deployed an interim force (United Nations Interim Forces in Lebanon or **UNIFIL**) which stationed peacekeeping troops as far north as the Litani River. The U.N. forces temporarily put a stop to Palestinian attacks but they could not keep the peace indefinitely. Terrorist activity resumed soon after the June ceasefire had been declared.

When a Palestinian terrorist group led by **Abu Nidal** attempted to assassinate Israel's Ambassador to Great Britain on June 3, 1982, the Israelis under the command of then-Defense Minister **Ariel Sharon** made a final attempt to drive the PLO out of the country. In the course of **"Operation Peace for Galilee,"** Israeli troops with the support of the united Christian Lebanese force (the

Phalangists)[32] overran PLO positions in southern Lebanon and engaged the Syrians (who had sided with the PLO) in an air confrontation. The PLO forces retreated to west Beirut (Lebanon's capital) where the siege continued.

Unable to withstand the barrage of attacks on PLO positions in the city by the combined forces of the Israeli Defense Force and the Lebanese Phalangists, the PLO surrendered and agreed to vacate Lebanon. By September 1982, more than 14,000 guerrillas had relocated to other Arab countries or to urban refugee camps outside the city (particularly **Sabra** and **Shatila**), and the PLO head-quarters was moved once again to the city of Tunis in Tunisia.

In mid-September, about the same time Lebanon's newly-elected Christian president **Bashir Gemayal** was assassinated, the Israelis decided to establish control over West Beirut and the suburb refugee towns of Sabra and Shatila (which were believed to contain bunkers, arsenals and command centers) by ridding the cities of all terrorists. To accomplish this, the Israelis agreed to sur-round and close off the Palestinian neighborhoods while Lebanese Christian Phalangists routed out rogue guerrillas. Instead, the Phalangists took the oppor-tunity to settle old scores and avenge Gemayal's murder by engaging in a bru-tal massacre of hundreds of Palestinian men, women and children.

The massacre was heavily criticized internationally with the greatest blame being put on the Israeli soldiers who had failed to prevent the atrocities. News of the onslaught was also met with widespread criticism from within Israel. For the first time in the nation's history, thousands of Israelis demonstrated against their own government's actions. As a result of the discord, **Menachim Begin**, Israeli's Prime Minister since 1977, resigned.

A peace agreement signed on May 17, 1983, ended the war between Lebanon and Israel but it didn't bring peace to Lebanon or to Israel. Despite the expul-sion of the PLO, the Phalangists were not strong enough to end terrorist activ-ity or keep the country's rival factions from fighting each other. The civil war in Lebanon resumed at the end of the summer and the terrorists, including a new radical Shi'ite organization based in Lebanon called **Hezbollah**, continued to harass Israel.

Israel retained a controversial security zone in south Lebanon as a buffer.

---

[32] By supporting the Christians, Israel's Secretary of Defense, Ariel Sharon, was also hoping to facilitate the creation of a Christian regime in Lebanon that would ally itself with Israel.

INTIFADA

On December 8, 1987, the simmering frustration felt by Palestinians crowded in the Gaza Strip under Israeli rule came to a head. On that day, an otherwise benign traffic accident, during which four Palestinians were killed in a collision with an Israeli truck, turned into a mass uprising. The incident drew an angry crowd and provoked an 18-year old Palestinian to throw a stone at some Israeli soldiers. When the soldiers fired back, the boy was killed thus inciting greater fury among the local Palestinians. To channel the rage, a group of activists circulated pamphlets calling for insurrection.

The ensuing *intifada* ("uprising") provoked Palestinian men, women and children to resist Israeli authority by refusing to pay taxes, boycotting Israeli products, conducting general strikes and, most disturbingly to the Israelis, to battle Israel's military forces with whatever weapons were available to them (rocks, bricks, molotov cocktails etc.)

The *intifada* quickly spread from the Gaza Strip to the West Bank and was embraced by all-sectors of Palestinians from refugee camps in Lebanon, Syria and Jordan as well as within Israel.

Although the PLO, then in exile in Tunis, was not the instigator of this rebellion, the organization's military leaders took control of the uprising and shaped it into a political instrument.

The Israelis, in the meantime, were in a difficult position knowing that armed responses to stone-throwers would create unfavorable publicity – which they could ill afford after the massacres at **Shatila** and **Sabra** in Lebanon. To quell the uprisings, therefore, Israeli soldiers resorted to using tear gas, shooting insurgents with rubber bullets or beating them with clubs or their hands. Still, images of heavily-armed soldiers defending themselves against the aggressions of destitute, young[33] Palestinians severely damaged Israel's image.

These demonstrations of Palestinian discontent along with the negative press generated over Israel's harsh reprisals shifted the world's sympathies in favor of the Palestinians. The newfound support inspired Yasser Arafat to seize this opportunity to advance the PLO's standing.

In order to win international support and recognition, the PLO leader announced that he was ready to recognize Israel's right to exist and, at a U.N. convention in December 1988, and a U.S. press conference, he declared that the PLO renounced violence in all its forms.

Israel's leaders, who maintained that they would never negotiate with PLO terrorists, were not swayed - nor were hard-line Palestinians.

Arafat's declaration was seen as traitorous by members of the **PFLP**[34] and the newly-formed **Hamas** organization (both committed to Islamic rule for all of Palestine) as well as by other radicals who vowed to do whatever they could to sabotage future Palestinian compromises.

---

[33] Most of the rebels were under the age of sixteen.

[34] The PFLP or the Popular Democratic Front for the Liberation of Palestine was formed in 1967 by Arab Nationalists as a counterweight to Arafat's Fatah organization.

GULF WAR

Peace talks between Palestinians and Israelis had been going along slowly since the **Yom Kippur War** in 1973, but it was Iraq's bold attack on its neighbor Kuwait in 1991 that finally pushed the parties into serious negotiations.

On August 2nd, 1990, Iraq's president, **Saddam Hussein**, sent his army into Kuwait in hopes that the move would draw attention away from Iraq's economic problems after 8-years of war with its neighbor, Iran[35]. The move was severely criticized internationally by Arab as well as Western countries. Saddam's only supporters, Libya, Sudan and the PLO were badly outnumbered by the U.S.-led coalition of 34 countries.

In order to maintain good-will among the coalition states (which included many Arab countries such as Syria, Egypt and Saudi Arabia), Israel was advised by the coalition to stay out of the conflict and to refrain from retaliating if the Iraqis attacked.

In order to win support from the Arab states, meanwhile, Saddam Hussein tried to make his act of aggression appear to be a political attack against Zionist imperialism. In an attempt to provoke Israel into entering the war (which would have immediately turned the battle into an Arab-Israeli conflict the Iraqi president was looking for), Hussein fired a number of random scud missiles at Israel's largest cities.

Israel, as instructed, suffered the blows stoically without returning a single shot – even though some of the missiles were believed to contain chemical weapons.

The war, which ended with Iraq's defeat in 1991, vividly exposed Israel's vulnerability to attacks by enemies at a distance as well as near its borders and strengthened Israel's desire for peace.

At the same time, the PLO's ill-fated alliance with Saddam Hussein had isolated the organization diplomatically. Some of the PLO's biggest supporters (Saudi Arabia and Kuwait particularly) cut off financial support and expelled Palestinians living within their borders. After the Gulf War, Yasser Arafat realized it was in his best interests to accelerate negotiations with Israel in order to build up his own prestige.

---

[35] After Iraq's war with Iran, the country's economy was in shambles and its oil-producing capabilities had been badly damaged. Iraq also owed millions of dollars to a number of Arab countries, including Kuwait, that it couldn't repay. (See Roraback, Amanda *Iraq in a Nutshell*, Enisen Publishing, 2002 for more details)

PEACE TREATIES

Camp David

After its near defeat in the Yom Kippur War, Israel was anxious to make peace with its Arab neighbors. In June 1977, therefore, Israeli Prime Minister **Menachem Begin** called on the leaders of Jordan, Syria and Egypt to discuss an end to conflict. Only President **Anwar Sadat** accepted Begin's olive branch by visiting Israel in November of that year.

Sadat realized that Egypt's ongoing state of war with Israel (which had begun in 1948 and resulted in the loss of the Sinai Peninsula in 1967 and defeat in 1973) was only draining resources from his already poor nation without bringing Israel any closer to collapse.

It was this realization as well as Sadat's belief that he was championing the cause of all Arab states and the Palestinians, which led to the Egyptian president's historic visit to address the Israeli Knesset (Parliament) on November 19, 1977.[36] Israel's Prime Minister, Menachem Begin, reciprocated the friendly gesture by visiting Egypt.

Peace talks between the two nations were carried out sporadically in 1977 and 1978. When a deadlock was reached, American President **Jimmy Carter** stepped in to mediate negotiations by inviting the leaders to a summit meeting at **Camp David**, a presidential retreat in Maryland, U.S.A.

The 12-day secret negotiations concluded with the signing of the **Treaty of Washington** ending the 31-year state of war between Israel and Egypt.

Under the terms of the treaty, Israel agreed to withdraw from the Sinai Peninsula within three years and dismantle military bases near the Gulf of Aqaba and the city of Yamit. Egypt, in return, promised to restore full diplomatic relations with Israel and granted Israeli ships free passage through the Suez Canal, the Tiran Straits and the Gulf of Aqaba. The peace between Israel and Egypt was celebrated in the West and earned the participants (Sadat and Begin) the 1978 Nobel Peace prize.[37] The Arab world, however, criticized Egypt for undermining Arab unity.

In Sadat's mind, the agreement was not simply a bilateral negotiation between Egypt and Israel exclusively but a first step towards a "just, comprehensive and durable settlement of the Middle East conflict." In line with his thinking, another series of peace talks were scheduled to take place within the year to discuss the Palestinian question.

---

[36] The visit (the first by an Arab leader to the state of Israel) earned Sadat the accolade of "Man of the Year for 1977" by *Time Magazine*.

[37] Jimmy Carter won a Nobel Peace Prize in 2002 for his work towards finding peaceful solutions to international conflicts.

Israel in a Nutshell

The second part of the treaty provided for an autonomous Palestinian regime in the West Bank and Gaza Strip for five years. The proposal (which was made without consulting the Palestinians) was overwhelmingly rejected by the PLO and the Arab states who viewed Egypt's recognition of Israel as a state a traitorous betrayal of pan-Arab aims. In opposition, the Arab states suspended Egypt's membership in the **Arab League** (a voluntary association of independent Arab-speaking countries) and cut off diplomatic relations.[38]

Without the benefit of Egypt's military muscle, the balance of power in the Middle East sharply shifted toward Israel as was revealed by Israel's victory over the Palestinians in Lebanon in 1982 and the subsequent expulsion of the PLO.

Lacking the strength of a "united Arab front," moreover, the Palestinians were forced to reformulate their objective from seeking "a national authority" in liberated Palestine to a more diplomatically acceptable goal of establishing an independent Palestinian state in the West Bank and Gaza Strip. The two-state solution indirectly implied Palestinian recognition of the state of Israel.

As PLO chairman and with world opinion behind him at the onset of the 1987 *intifada*, **Yasser Arafat** took the opportunity to address the United Nations to announce the PLO's new stance on the status of Israel as well as the organization's acceptance of **UN resolution 242** (which called on Israel to withdraw from territories seized in the 1967 war). Arafat also publicly denounced the use of terrorism.

Much to the dismay of the Israelis who vowed never to negotiate with known "terrorists," the United States responded to Arafat's overtures by announcing that the U.S. was ready to conduct talks with the PLO.

Relations between the U.S. and the PLO soured, however, in 1990, when the PLO failed to condemn a Palestinian attack in Tel Aviv and when it became clear that the Palestinians would not accept Palestinian autonomy (self-government within Israel) rather than independent statehood. Arafat's support for Iraqi dictator **Saddam Hussein** during the 1991 Gulf War further damaged relations between the Palestinians and the West and isolated Arafat from the rest of the Arab nations who condemned Hussein's seizure of Kuwait as a violation of that small Arab state's sovereign rights.

To repel the Iraqi invaders, the U.S. formed a coalition of Western and Arab states -- excluding the PLO and, to avoid antagonizing the Arab coalition forces, Israel. Israel's promise of non-participation left it vulnerable to attacks by Hussein who tried to provoke Israel into entering the war by firing indiscriminately aimed scud missiles into Tel Aviv. If Israel became involved in the war, Hussein hoped, the conflict could be turned into an Israeli-Arab confrontation which would compel the Arab states to drop their support of the west in favor of Arabic Iraq. But the Israelis kept their promise of non-involvement and held back retaliatory fire.

---

[38] Diplomatic relations with Egypt were restored in 1987 and the nation was readmitted to the league in 1989.

Madrid

The damage in Tel Aviv caused by Iraq in the course of the Gulf War vividly exposed Israel's vulnerability to attack not only from within its borders but attacks directed by antagonistic Arab nations further afield. The feeling of defenselessness(coupled with defeats in the Yom Kippur War and in Lebanon) compelled Israel to revisit the peace process.

The PLO, in the meantime, had suffered serious setbacks both internally (with the assassination of two out of three of its top leaders) and internationally due to Arafat's unpopular support of the Iraqi dictator.

For the West, the war highlighted the need to put an end to the Arab-Israeli conflict which lay behind all Middle-East affairs.

Shortly after the 1991 Iraq War, U.S. President **George Bush** (senior) sent his Secretary of State, **James Baker**, to the Middle East to persuade Israel and neighboring Arab states to attend a peace conference cosponsored by the United States and the U.S.S.R.. Israeli Prime Minister **Yitzhak Shamir** agreed to attend the talks on the condition that the PLO would not be permitted to participate. Shamir's participation also depended on U.S. willingness to guarantee a loan for Israel of ten billion dollars to help deal with the influx of Soviet Jewish immigrants (who flooded Israel after the 1991 collapse of the U.S.S.R.).[39] Shamir further demanded that the peace talks be implemented in two parts with negotiations being made between Israel and each individual Arab state and then separate talks between Israel and the Palestinians. Lastly, Shamir insisted that negotiations with the Palestinians be aimed at reaching an interim arrangement of "self-government" (as opposed to statehood) as outlined in the Camp David Accords.

Despite the fact that the talks were not designed to deal with the refugee problem, promote the creation of a Palestinian state nor did they involved direct participation by the PLO, Arafat encouraged non-PLO Palestinian delegates (pending his personal approval) to attend the negotiations in order to ensure Palestinian representation (absent at the Camp David Accords).

The peace conference began in **Madrid**, Spain on October 30, 1991, and brought Israel's Prime Minister together with delegates from Syria, Lebanon, Jordan and Egypt. Most significantly, this was the first Israeli-Arab assembly that including the participation of Palestinians as a separate entity with a unique national identity.[40]

The October/November talks ended without any settlements but all parties expressed interest in continuing the peace process. For the next few months,

---

[39] **George Bush** opposed giving loans to Israel since the funds were often used to pay for the construction of controversial settlements.

[40] Palestinians were previously considered Arabs whose identity was determined by the countries in which they resided (i.e. Jordanians, Egyptians and Lebanese etc.). The Israelis had denied that a unique "Palestinian" identity existed.

talks dragged on haltingly[41] in Washington DC and survived a shift in leadership in both the United States and Israel.

In October, 1992, the Israelis elected a new Prime Minister, **Yitzhak Rabin**, from the milder **Labour Party**, who promised to bring peace to Israel within a year. In the U.S. **George H. Bush** was defeated in the November 1992 presidential elections by **Bill Clinton**, who was known to have stronger sympathies towards Israel than his predecessor.

Late in 1992, the kidnapping and murder of an Israeli police officer by the militant Palestinian group, **Hamas,** and Israel's deportation of 415 suspected Hamas activists in retribution prompted the Palestinian delegates to walk out of the conference in opposition to Israel's actions. Without Palestinian representatives, the talks were brought to a standstill.

After ten rounds of disrupted negotiations, the delegates had reached an impasse over the most important issues: the status of Jerusalem, Israeli settlements, land and water rights and the fate of the Palestinian refugees. The participants at this point were only going through the motions when another series of secret exploratory talks began to take place in Oslo, Norway.

Oslo Accords

The Oslo Talks began as a clandestine meeting between a PLO representative, an Israeli professor with connections to Israel's Labour government and (as a cover) a Norwegian social scientist who assembled to discuss the issues that were sidestepped at the Washington talks.

At the first meeting, the delegates agreed to set aside the most difficult issues (for example the status of Jerusalem) until later and immediately focused on less contentious issues. At this meeting, the Israeli delegates agreed to give up control over the volatile Gaza Strip, which the Israelis were happy to surrender. Back at the PLO headquarters in Tunis, Arafat gladly accepted Gaza and asked for the city of Jericho as well (to give him a foothold in the West Bank).

After informing Israel's Prime Minister Rabin that the talks were taking place, the delegates met a second time. At this meeting, the representatives drew up a first draft of the "**Declaration of Principles.**"

Although the initial "Declaration" still required amendments, the relatively rapid progress of the Oslo meetings in comparison to the slow-moving official peace talks taking place in Washington appealed to both the Israelis and Palestinians who were looking for a timely resolution to the Israeli-Palestinian conflict.

The PLO was suffering economically due to the loss of its biggest benefactors:

---

[41] It was believed that Yitzhak Shamir hoped to delay the peace agreement for ten years -- long enough to build sufficient Israeli settlements in the Palestinian territories (called "facts on the ground") to make Israeli possession of the land a *fait accompli*.

the Soviet Union, which had collapsed in 1991, and the oil-producing Gulf States that had withdrawn support because of Arafat's relationship with Saddam Hussein. The PLO was also anxious to restore its regional authority which had declined after its failure to turn the *intifada* into a powerful political tool and the subsequent rise of competitive Islamic fundamentalists (See "Hamas" in Palestine section).

The Israelis were eager to solve the Palestinian problem and bring an end to the *intifada*, which required costly military expenditures to subdue and had cost Israel great amounts of money in lost revenues due to the boycott of Israeli products. They were also anxious to prevent a future uprising and to end Israel's political and economic isolation from the rest of the Arab world.

After a last **Oslo** session on August 11, 1993, the parties came to a settlement and penned a final "Declaration of Principles." A month later, Israeli Prime Minister Yitzhak Rabin and PLO Chairman Yasser Arafat sealed the agreement with a historic handshake in Washington D.C. on the White House lawn. For their efforts, both Arafat and Rabin as well as Israel's Foreign Minister, Shimon Peres, were awarded Nobel Peace prizes.

According to the terms of the "Declaration of Principles," Israel agreed to withdraw from the Gaza Strip and Jericho with further withdrawals to take place within the following five years. Gaza and the West Bank would be granted self-rule under an Interim Government Authority (the **Palestinian Authority** headed by Yasser Arafat) in the transitional period not to exceed five years, leading to a permanent settlement based on **UN Security Council Resolutions 242 and 338.**

Along with "the transition of authority from the Israeli military government and its Civil Administration to the authorized Palestinians, authority would be transferred to the Palestinians in the following spheres: education and culture, health, social welfare, direct taxation and tourism." The Palestinians were also responsible for building a police force with light weapons (Israel would maintain responsibility for security against external threats) and establishing a number of divisions including: a Palestinian Electricity Authority, a Gaza Sea Port Authority, a Palestinian Development Bank and other offices. In order to fund these new programs, the United States convened a Donors Conference to solicit contributions that was attended by delegates from 43 nations[42].

Future negotiations were scheduled to begin "no later than the beginning of the third year of the [5-year] interim period" to decide the remaining issues which included: Jerusalem, refugees, settlements, security arrangements, borders and relations with neighboring countries.

The Oslo Accord was celebrated as a first step towards peace in the Middle East and inspired Jordan to sign an agreement ending forty-six years of war; however, it did not bring peace to the area.

The fulfillment of the "Declaration of Principles" was scheduled for 1999 but a number of setbacks delayed its realization. The Israelis were reluctant to relinquish control to the PLO and Palestinians who opposed the treaty (especially members of the militant groups Hamas and Islamic Jihad) attempted to derail the agreement through violent attacks.

Israelis feared that a return to pre-1967 borders would place some of its biggest industries and populated cities just miles away from belligerent Palestinians and the possibility that Islamic radicals could wrest control of the PLO by assassinating Arafat (himself vilified as a terrorist by many Israelis) was also a concern.

Palestinian opponents to the peace treaties believed that Arafat had traded Palestinian rights to Israel to bolster recognition of his own leadership. By agreeing to the two-state compromise, moreover, some Palestinians felt Arafat was, in effect, accepting Israel's claim to land that it had illegally occupied at the expense of hundreds of thousands of refugees. Palestinian anger was further inflamed in 1994 when a Jewish settler (Baruch Goldstein) opened fire in the crowded Ibrahimi Mosque in Hebron killing 29 Muslims as they prayed and wounding more than 100 more. The massacre was immediately followed by riots and PLO rivals who were not bound by the directives of the treaty (which prohibited terrorism) continued to fight for complete control of Palestine. Throughout 1994 and 1995, dozens of Israeli civilians were killed in attacks by extremists from Hamas and Islamic Jihad.

In spite of the bloodshed, the Israelis began to withdraw from Gaza and Jericho on May 18, 1994, and Arafat and the PLO returned to Palestine for the first time in 33 years to take the reins of the Palestinian Authority. For the next few months Israel transferred control of education, culture, health care, social welfare, taxation and tourism to the Palestinians (as decreed in the "Declaration of Principles"). Israel moved its troops in the Gaza and Jericho to protect the settlements.

---

[42] The U.S. promised to donate $500 million over 5-years, Israel pledged $25 million and a loan of $50 million, Japan offered $200 million over 2 years, the Saudis, $100 million for the first year etc.

Oslo II

In September, 1995, Israeli and Palestinian delegates returned to the bargaining table to finalize the second round of peace agreements. Oslo II, signed officially in Washington D.C. on September 28, 1995, expanded the area of Palestinian self-rule beyond Gaza and Jericho to include the cities of Bethlehem, Jenin, Nablus, Qalqilya and Tulkarm in the West Bank. The Israeli Civil Administration was to cede authority to an 82-member Palestinian council to be elected for 5-years that would govern Gaza and the West Bank. Special status would be granted to the city of Hebron[43] where Israeli soldiers would remain to protect Israeli settlers.

The peace treaty was criticized by some members of the Israeli right who felt that the Prime Minister was giving away land that Israelis had spent the last half century struggling to reclaim. Two months after signing Oslo II, one of these extremists took matters into his own hands by assassinating Israel's Prime Minister, **Yitzhak Rabin**, moments after he had attended a peace rally in Tel Aviv.

The murder was a terrible blow, not only to Israelis but to the international community. It was akin to the killing of American president John F. Kennedy in Dallas, Texas. Rabin's funeral was attended by statesmen from around the world including American President Bill Clinton, British Prime Minister John Majors, German Chancellor Helmut Kohl, Egyptian President Hosni Mubarak and other European and Arab dignitaries. Even Yasser Arafat and King Hussein of Jordan sent heartfelt condolences.

Rabin's replacement, **Shimon Peres**, promised to go forward with the peace plan and fulfill the promises made by his predecessor (including the withdrawal from the Golan Heights on the border with Syria), but his pacifist posture concerned Israeli conservatives.

The Palestinians, meanwhile, held elections on January 20, 1996, to decide who would be the first president of the new **Palestinian Authority**. Not surprisingly, Yasser Arafat won in a landslide victory. But continued Palestinian attacks in Hebron and the Gaza Strip (including a bomb detonated by a Hamas militant in a Jerusalem bus that killed 25 people), created doubt among the Israelis that Arafat was capable or willing to rein in Muslim extremists and end the Palestinian violence. In response to the attacks, Peres decided to postpone Israeli withdrawal from the city of Hebron.

---

[43] Hebron is home to the Cave of Macphelah and the Ibrahimi Mosque (built over the cave) where Adam and Eve, Abraham and Sarah, Isaac, Ishmael, Jacob and their wives are believed to have been buried. The site is sacred to Jews and Muslims and has been an area of contention for centuries. Before 1967, the Arabs prohibited Jews from entering the tombs. After the 1967 Six-Day War and Israel's acquisition of the West Bank, Jewish access was permitted and administration of the shrine remained in Muslim hands.

Since the late 19th century, the city's population has been overwhelmingly Palestinian. Beginning in 1972, however, a number of extremist Israelis settled in Hebron provoking much unrest in the city. The 400-strong Hebron settlement community was guarded by more than 2000 Israeli soldiers.

As Palestinian violence continued, Israelis became increasingly concerned for their safety. In the October, 1996 elections, therefore, voters replaced Peres with a militant politician from the conservative Likud Party, **Benjamin Netanyahu.**

The assumption of power by this extreme right-wing leader and critic of the Oslo treaty, shattered the Palestinians' hopes of creating an independent Palestinian state in the West Bank and Gaza. Netanyahu suspended the phased Israeli withdrawal from the West Bank, sped up the construction of Jewish settlements in disputed lands[44] (the Oslo Agreement didn't include any calls for a freeze on construction of Israeli settlements) and advocated opening a tunnel for archaeological purposes along the western foundation of the sacred Al-Aqsa Mosque. The Prime Minister also ordered the assassination of leaders of Hamas.

In order to help speed up the promised Israeli evacuation from Hebron and other West Bank cities, U.S. Secretary of State Madeleine Albright visited Netanyahu to coerce him into withdrawing from an additional 13% of the West Bank within a predetermined time-frame. To seek leverage with the West by appearing to be the true proponent for peace against the Israel's reluctant prime minister, Yasser Arafat agreed to the 13% withdrawal plan. The arrangement was later stymied by members of the U.S. Congress who warned President Clinton that forcing a withdrawal would damage the peace process.

The Palestinians, meanwhile, were accused by Netanyahu of violating the peace agreement themselves by failing to dismantle radical groups like Hamas, not reducing the police force to the level fixed in the Oslo Accords and by stockpiling forbidden weapons (machine guns, anti-tank missiles etc.).

Wye Treaty

To try to salvage the floundering Oslo Peace Agreements, President **Clinton** called on Netanyahu and Yasser Arafat to attend a conference at the **Wye River Plantation** in Maryland, U.S.A.

An agreement was signed nine days later obligating Israel to expand the territory that was under Palestinian control and release 750 political prisoners. Discussions would be conducted regarding the opening of an airport in Gaza and the establishment of corridors of safe passage between Gaza and the West Bank. Israel also agreed to reunite Palestinian families that were living on opposite sides of the *green line* and to permit students to travel freely between the West Bank and Gaza.

In return, the Palestinians agreed to formally remove an article in the PLO Covenant of 1968 that called for the destruction of Israel[45] and promised to

---

[44] While the U.S. and Israel use the phrase "disputed land" to describe the West Bank and Gaza Strip areas, Palestinians prefer the term "occupied."

[45] In December 1998, U.S. President Bill Clinton made a historic trip to Gaza to witness the revision of the PLO Covenant.

take all measures necessary to prevent hostile attacks on Israeli citizens by arresting Palestinian terrorists and dismantling terrorist organizations.

While some movement was made towards fulfilling the terms of the Wye agreement, the peace process was again disrupted by perceived violations on both sides. The Palestinians complained that the Israelis had released petty criminals among the 750 prisoners rather than political prisoners deemed by the Israelis to have "blood on their hands." The Israelis argued that although they had faithfully given up territory to the Palestinians, the PLO hadn't made any effort to prevent terrorist attacks or take measures to dismantle militant Islamic groups. Moreover, Yasser Arafat threatened to unilaterally declare the establishment of a Palestinian state on May 4, 1999, the date when negotiations were scheduled to end according to the Oslo Treaty.[46] In revenge, Netanyahu threatened to cancel future removal of troops from Palestinian territory.

Netanyahu's failure to bring a final resolution to the peace process eventually led to the collapse of his government. In the May 1999 Israeli elections, Netanyahu was overwhelmingly defeated by the Labour Party's candidate **Ehud Barak**.

Barak's first priority upon assuming the office of Prime Minister was to broker a peace agreement with Syria over the controversial Golan Heights which Israel had incorporated within its borders in 1967. When he found that an agreement wasn't negotiable, he turned his attention back to the Palestinian issue by promising to reinvigorate the peace treaty.

The Palestinians, in the meantime, were angered by the continued construction of Israeli settlements in the occupied areas and the development of a network of walled highways connecting the settlements to Israeli cities through Palestinian-inhabited territory. Palestinians feared these settlements were designed to claim an increasing portion of Palestinian territory in order to make land division impossible.

Camp David II

President Clinton believed that with Ehud Barak as Prime Minister of Israel he could get the Oslo agreement back on track. In July, 2000, therefore, the American President invited Barak and Yasser Arafat to Camp David to try to reach an agreement on the long-overdue final status of the Oslo Treaty.

However, both the Israelis and the Palestinians came to the table with demands that were unacceptable to the other party. Barak proclaimed a number of "red lines" that he would not cross: 1. East Jerusalem must remain under Israeli sov-

---

[46] Many Israelis feared that a Palestinian state could become a staging ground for violence against Israelis -- potentially also allowing other belligerent Arab states to station troops near the Israeli border. On the other hand, the Palestinians and Israelis were already intertwined economically. The Israelis relied on the Palestinian labor force while the Palestinians relied on Israel for employment and the flow of goods between the spheres connected the Israelis and Palestinians commercially.

ereignty, 2. Israel would not return to the limits of the 1967 borders, 3. Israel would not accept moral or legal responsibility for the Palestinian refugee status nor agree to a "right of return" by the Palestinians to areas they had "evacuated" in 1948[47] and lastly, 4. Israel was entitled to annex settlement blocs in Judea and Samaria[48] (thereby limiting Israeli withdrawal from parts of the West Bank).

Arafat, for his part, insisted that 1. Palestinians had sole sovereignty over the Noble Sanctuary (the "Temple Mount" to the Jews), 2. that U.N. Resolution 242, which required Israel to withdraw to its pre-1967 borders, should be fulfilled in its entirety, 3. that according to the terms set forth in U.N. Resolution 194 ("The Right of Return") Israel was obligated to allow all Palestinian refugees to return to the homes they were forced to abandon in the course of the 1948 and 1967 wars or be compensated for the property that was lost, and 4. Israel must withdraw from the Gaza Strip and the vast majority of the West Bank (including Jerusalem) as agreed in the Oslo Treaties.

The vastly divergent requirements left little room for compromise. Consequently, the Camp David II talks ended after 15 days with no agreement.

Second or "Al-Aqsa"[49] Intifada

The failures of the peace treaties to address and resolve issues that were daily affecting the Palestinians increasingly frustrated the population of refugees living in the West Bank and Gaza. None of the agreements tackled the "right of return," for example, or dealt with the humiliating Israeli guarded border-crossings. Nor had they curbed the construction of Israeli settlements (which nearly doubled in number during the 1990s).[50] Israelis still monopolized trade, investment and water resources and, by the year 2000, the living standard among Palestinians had dropped by 30% with a 50% unemployment rate. The peace treaties appeared to have benefited Israel and Arafat personally with little regard to the Palestinian plight.

In such an unstable atmosphere, therefore, it was no surprise that a visit to the sacred Noble Sanctuary by a prominent Jewish politician could unleash such a torrent of violence. On September 28, 2000, **Ariel Sharon**, the leader of the opposition Likud Party at that time and, Palestinians believed, the man responsible for the 1982 massacre of several hundred Palestinians in the Lebanese **Sabra** and **Shatila** refugee camp,[51] decided to visit the Muslim's most holy site

[47] Barak (as others who fear the return of refugees) believed that the repatriation of four million Palestinian refugees would quickly bring an end to the state of Israel

[48] Israelis refer to the "West Bank" as "Judea and Samaria," after the ancient Hebrew provinces that once flourished in the area.

[49] The Al-Aqsa Mosque sits upon the Noble Sanctuary commemorating Mohammed's ascension to heaven.

[50] Palestinians believed that the Israelis were underhandedly trying to offset territorial losses mandated in the Oslo Treaty by expanding Israel proper through Jewish settlements and their surrounding "buffer zones."

[51] Israelis say that it was not then-Defense Minister Ariel Sharon but the Lebanese Phalangists who committed the atrocities.

in Palestine, the Noble Sanctuary, accompanied by a thousand policemen.

Sharon claimed that his visit was not meant to provoke Palestinians but was intended as a gesture of peace. It was explained that the move exhibited the right of religious freedom enjoyed by all citizens, a right that allows unlimited access to all holy sites, Muslim, Christian or Jewish.

The Palestinians, on the other hand, viewed the move as a calculated provocation designed to pander to the Jewish extremists, to claim Israel's sovereignty over the holy site and to prevent the further continuation of peace talks.

Moments after Sharon had left the site, hundreds of Palestinians began to throw rocks at Israeli police. A day later, a demonstration was staged which turned into guerrilla attacks. The Israelis responded initially by firing rubber bullets at the demonstrators and later matched the escalation of violence by employing tanks, gunships and jet fighters to suppress the Palestinians. Far more violent than the 1987-1991 uprising, the 2000 Al-Aqsa *intifada* took the lives of more than 1,500 Palestinians and 500 Israelis. On the Palestinian side, an internationally broadcast image of a 12-year old boy being sheltered by his father in a barrage of bullets (the Palestinian boy was killed in the crossfire) demonstrated Palestinian vulnerability, while the lynching of two Israeli reservists in Ramallah reflected a deep-seated Palestinian hatred of the Jews. This led Israelis to call for greater security measures and to request the removal of Israel's dovish Prime Minister, Ehud Barak.

In March 2001, Ariel Sharon formally replaced Ehud Barak as Israel's prime minister. A month later, the new leader launched a full-scale invasion of Palestinian territory thereby intensifying the cycle of violence that had begun with the 2000 *intifada*.

Since the onset of the uprising, Palestinian suicide ("martyr") attacks had greatly increased in frequency and were carried out by a new class of Palestinians. Earlier, militants were typically single men between the ages of 17 and 23. Since the September *intifada*, though, "martyrs" could be poor or wealthy, middle-aged or young, single or married men or women with or without children. At times bombers would disguise themselves as Israeli soldiers, orthodox Jews or even pregnant women with explosives strapped to their stomachs in order to gain entry into crowded Israeli venues without detection. The target areas were seemingly randomly chosen among locales with large concentrations of Jews including shopping malls, restaurants, coffee houses, pool halls and crowded buses leaving the population in a constant state of insecurity and terror.

With each attack, the Sharon government retaliated by raiding refugee camps and occupying Palestinian cities in the West Bank and Gaza Strip. Ariel Sharon also ordered the assassination (without trial) of a number of militant leaders believed to have been involved in attacks on Israeli citizens. In April, 2001, for example, Israelis assassinated an Islamic Jihad commander in the Gaza strip. In August, 2001, the leader of the Popular Front for the Liberation of Palestine (PFLP) was killed in an Israeli shell attack. In November, 2001, Israelis assassinated the most senior Hamas militant on its wanted list and in January, 2002, **Raed al-Karmi**, a Palestinian leader in the al-Aqsa Brigades, was killed. In some cases, Sharon also targeted the families of suicide bombers and militants by ordering Israeli troops to destroy their homes[52] and threatening to deport the relatives of Palestinian terrorists.

In the latest chapter of a 20-year old feud between Ariel Sharon and Yasser Arafat that had begun with then-defense minister Sharon's command over Israeli tanks that laid siege to Arafat's headquarters in Lebanon in 1982,[53] Prime Minister Sharon pledged to bring about the destruction of his Palestinian rival - if not physically, then psychologically and politically.

For months, Arafat was confined by Israeli troops to his compound in **Ramallah**, forbidden even to attend an Arab League meeting to discuss the terms of a Saudi Arabian peace proposal. In March 2002, in what Sharon called the first stage of a "long and complicated war that knows no border," Israeli tanks and bulldozers were poised to demolish Arafat's Ramallah compound prompting the PLO leader to proclaim in defiance that he would rather die than surrender or live in exile.

Sharon's hard-line stance against Palestinian violence (which he countered by redeploying troops within Palestinian territory) was accompanied by a radically stepped-up pace of construction projects to establish Israeli settlements in the West Bank and Gaza. A small settlement with a few hundred Israeli inhabitants justified the presence of thousands of Israeli troops posted near the settlements to protect the residents. The Israeli soldiers, in turn, could keep an eye on potential belligerent activity within Palestinian territory.

Road Map

Two years into the deadly conflict between Arafat and the Palestinians and Sharon and his Israeli supporters, American President **George W. Bush** reintroduced America's role as Middle East peace mediator.

The attack on New York's World Trade Center on **September 11, 2001** prompted George Bush to declare an international "war on terrorism" and directed worldwide attention once again to the yet unsolved Israeli-Palestinian problem that stood at the core of the unstable relationship between the West and the Arab/Muslim countries.

In a speech on June 24, 2002, George Bush stated that it was "untenable for Israeli citizens to live in terror and untenable for Palestinians to live in squalor and occupation." In lieu of this destructive state of affairs, Bush envisioned the creation of two states (Palestine and Israel) divided along the pre-1967 borders and living side by side in peace and security. The viability of such a Palestinian

---

[52] Ariel Sharon has been nicknamed "the Bulldozer" by Israelis.

[53] Sharon told an Israeli newspaper that he regrets not having "liquidated" (killed) Arafat during the invasion.

state, he reasoned, would depend upon the establishment of a new Palestinian leadership based on tolerance and liberty, new courts and laws, a new constitution and the creation of a Palestinian parliament and, of course, the complete renunciation of terrorism. Israelis would have to cease settlement activity in the occupied areas and help resolve questions concerning the status of Jerusalem and the refugee problem.

These ideas became the principle tenets in a peace plan sponsored by a "quartet" of international entities (the United States, the European Union, Russia and the United Nations). The "Road Map for Peace," as the treaty was called, was divided into three phases with the ultimate goal of ending the conflict by the year 2005.

In the first phase (from October 2002 to May 2003), the Palestinian leadership was reformed with the appointment of a new Palestinian Cabinet, the creation of an Election committee and the establishment of an empowered prime minister. **Mahmoud Abbas**, also known as **Abu Mazen**, served as the Palestinian Authority's first prime minister from March 2003 until his resignation in September the same year.[54] The Palestinian leadership was also required to issue a statement "reiterating Israel's right to exist in peace and security and calling for an immediate end to the armed *intifada* and all acts of violence against Israelis anywhere."

The Israelis in the first phase of the peace plan were instructed to improve humanitarian conditions by lifting curfews, allowing ease of movement between Palestinian areas and by freezing all settlement expansions. The Israelis were also required to dismantle settlement outposts that had been erected since Sharon had come to power in 2000. By May 2002, a report by **B Tselem**, an Israeli human rights group, claimed that the Jewish state had secretly grabbed 42% of Palestinian land in the West Bank for illegal settlement activity.[55]

Based upon the approval of the **Quartet** (U.S., E.U., U.N. and Russia) the transitional **Phase II** (June 2003-December 2003) would begin after Palestinian elections and end with the possible creation of a Palestinian state with provisional borders in the year 2003. This goal would be accomplished only when the Palestinian people had a leadership that was acting against terror and which was willing and able to build a practicing democracy based on tolerance and liberty. Pre-*intifada* links to Israel would then be restored (trade offices etc.) and talks would begin to discuss regional water, environmental issues, economic development, refugees and arms control issues.

---

[54] Abbas and Arafat were engaged in a power struggle from the moment Abbas was reluctantly appointed prime minister by Palestinian Authority President Arafat in March 2003. Abbas finally resigned because he was denied control over the PA security forces. He was replaced by Ahmed Korei.

[55] According to the B'Tselem report, "Land Grab: Israel's Settlement Policy in the West Bank: issued in May 2002, settlements are built on 1.7% of the territory of the West Bank and control 41.9% of the land (including land designated as municipal boundaries and land assigned to Regional Councils).

If all requirements had been met, a meeting would be scheduled in **Phase III** (2004 to 2005) to negotiate a final permanent status agreement. At this stage, final border lines would be determined and negotiations would take place to decide the fate of Jerusalem, Palestinian refugees and Israeli settlements. Arab states would then be encouraged to accept normal relations with Israel and the state of Palestine would be accepted in the international community (including possible recognition in the United Nations).

Geneva Plan

Despite the efforts by the United States, the United Nations, the European Union and Russia to bring a lasting peace to the region, Israel and Palestine remained in a state of conflict. Israelis continued to colonize Gaza and the West Bank and Palestinian militants (who rejected all negotiated agreements and were beyond the purview of the Palestinian Authority) continued to attack Israeli civilians provoking harsh reprisals from Israel. Palestinians upheld their demands that Israel withdraw from all settlements built on Palestinian land, return to the pre-1967 border and permit all refugees to return to the homes they had abandoned in the course of the 1948 and 1967 wars.

Aggravating the conflict in 2002, the Israelis began constructing a separating wall along the *green line* dividing Israeli and Palestinian territory. Israelis said the fence was designed to keep out suicide bombers. Palestinians claimed the wall (which cut deep into territory occupied by Israel in 1967) was built to annex land.

Despite these obstacles, at the end of 2003 a group of influential Israelis and Palestinians (with no official authority) fashioned an alternative treaty to the declining "Quartet" road map that proposed a two-state solution to the Middle East crisis. The plan (called the "**Geneva Plan**") suggested imposing strict limits on the number of returning Palestinian refugees, designed a contiguous Palestinian state in the West Bank that would be connected to Gaza by a secure overland highway and advocated the end of excessive Israeli occupation of Palestinian lands while allowing more than half of the Israeli settlers to remain permanently in the West Bank.

The plan also included precise border delineations and solutions for the future of Jerusalem and its holy places including unrestricted access to the sites by specific routes.

The success of this plan (as all others) depends on the willingness and ability of the Israelis and Palestinians to compromise on their demands and resolve the differences within their own constituencies.

ISRAELI POLITICS

Israel's government is a parliamentary democracy with executive, legislative and judicial branches. Heading the government is the president, essentially a ceremonial position, who is elected by the **Knesset** (Israel's parliament) for a 5-year term. **Moshe Katsav** has held the post since July 2000. The president appoints superior court justices and signs treaties and laws enacted by the Knesset but does not have veto power over legislation.

The 120-member Knesset serves as Israel's legislative branch of government with exclusive authority to enact laws. The Knesset is elected by "general national, direct, equal, secret and proportional elections" - that is, every Israeli over the age of 18 chooses among lists of candidates from each party. Seats are distributed according to the proportion of votes each list received. For example, if the list of candidates presented by the Likud Party wins 30% of the vote, it is allotted 30% of the seats in the Knesset. The Likud party will then assign the first 36 people (or 30% of 120) from its list to sit in Israel's parliament.

Between 1996 and 2001, Israel's prime minister was elected by direct popular vote for a four-year term. Prior to 1996 and after 2001, the president has had the right to decide which party leader is most able to form a coalition government -- traditionally, the leader of the majority party. The prime minister, as the executive, is then responsible for appointing the governing cabinet including the posts of foreign minister, defense minister, finance minister etc. Ariel Sharon was elected prime minister in February 2001 and reelected in January 2003.

Israel has no formal constitution but governs according to guidelines presented in the Declaration of Independence, the Basic Laws of the Parliament and the Israeli Citizenship Law.

Labour (or Labor) Party
One of Israel's dominating parties; the social-democratic Labour Party was formed in 1968 by merging the left-wing parties of Mapai, Rafi and Ahdut Ha'avodah. The party advocates compromise with the Palestinians and favors the establishment of a Palestinian state. It also supports programs that promote full employment and other labor issues.

Likud (Unity) Party
The right-wing Likud Party, whose roots trace back to Jabotinsky (see "World War I"), emerged as a political party in 1977. Most of the party's members fervently oppose the creation of a Palestinian state and support Israeli settlements in the West Bank and Gaza Strip. Economically, the Likud Party promotes private ownership and capitalist free-market economics. Generally, hard-line Likud representatives have been voted into the Knesset during times of violence in the country.

POLITICAL PARTIES

Party	Support Base	% votes in 2003 elections
Likud		(29.4%) 38 seats
Labor		(14.5%) 19 seats
Religious Parties		
Shas	Low-income, Sephardic Jews	(8.2%) 11 seats
National Religious Party (NRP)		
	Middle-class, moderate	(4.2%) 6 seats
United Torah Judaism (UTJ)		
	Ultra-Orthodox Jews	(4.3%) 5 seats
Left-Wing		
Meretz		(5.2%) 6 seats
Right-Wing		
National Union		
	West Bank and Gaza settlers	(5.5%) 7 seats
Liberal Economic		
Shinui	Urban upper-middle classes	(12.3%) 15 seats
Immigrant Party		
Yisrael Beiteinu (merged with National Union)		
	Soviet immigrants	
Arab Party		
United Arab List		(2.1%) 2 seats

and other parties (Democratic Front for Peace and Equality, One Nation, National Democratic Alliance, Green Leaf Party, YBA, Herut etc.) making up the total 120 seats.

PRIME MINISTERS

Prime Ministers	Years in Power	Party Affiliation
David Ben-Gurion	(1948-54)	Labour
Moshe Sharett	(1954-55)	Labour
David Ben-Gurion	(1955-63)	Labour
Levi Eshkol	(1963-69)	Labour
Golda Meir	(1969-74)	Labour
Yitzhak Rabin	(1974-77)	Labour
Menachim Begin	(1977-83)	Likud
Yitzhak Shamir	(1983-84)	Likud
Shimon Peres	(1984-86)	Likud
Benjamin Netanyahu	(1996-99)	Likud
Ehud Barak	(1999-01)	Labour
Ariel Sharon	(2001-)	Likud

Ariel Sharon

In February 2001, Ariel Sharon was elected Israel's prime minister and was reelected in January 2003.

Before becoming prime minister, Sharon helped establish the Likud Party in 1973 and served as Yitzhak Rabin's special security adviser from 1975-1977.

As defense minister in 1982, Sharon orchestrated Israel's invasion of Lebanon which brought about the destruction of the PLO infrastructure in Lebanon. He was forced to resign in 1983, however, after being charged with failing to prevent the massacre of more than 2,000 Palestinians at the Sabra and Shatila refugee camps by Lebanese Christian militiamen.

From 1990-1992 Sharon served as the Minister of Construction and Housing and Chairman of the Ministerial Committee on Immigration and Absorption. In order to accommodate the waves of immigrants to Israel from Russia following the fall of the Soviet Union, Sharon oversaw the biggest building drive of Jewish settlements in the West Bank and Gaza since its occupation in the Six-Day War of 1967 while serving in this post.

Sharon became leader of the Likud Party in May 1999 and helped trigger the second Palestinians intifada by visiting the Temple Mount (Haram al-Sharif or Noble Sanctuary) in 2000.

As prime minister, Sharon has ordered the assassination of leaders of Palestinian militant groups, the destruction of houses of suspected terrorists, the confinement of Yasser Arafat in his headquarters in Ramallah and advocated the building of settlements in the West Bank and Gaza Strip. He has also met with Palestinian prime ministers and maintained that he is not interested in the collapse of the Palestinian authority or in taking over Palestinian cities.

REFUGEES

Moments after the creation of the independent state of Israel, a coalition of Arab states declared war on the new nation. In the course of the 1948 conflict, hundreds of thousands of "Palestinians"[56] heeded the advice of the Arab invaders to leave the territory -- despite Israeli guarantees of safety. [57] Most of the refugees fled to surrounding Arab countries where they were housed in temporary camps run by the **United Nations Relief and Works Agency** (UNRWA).

Rather than absorbing the Palestinian refugees into their countries, though, the Arab states (Jordan excluded) refused to integrate their Arab brothers into the populace in order to exploit them as political pawns in their fight against Israel. As long as the refugee crisis remained dire, it was reasoned, there was an urgent need to clear the area of Zionists and return the area to Arab rule. If Palestinians were absorbed into Syria, Lebanon or Egypt, on the other hand, the Palestinian issue would eventually disappear and the existence of Israel would become an internationally recognized fact.

As the Palestinian Arabs fled to neighboring countries, moreover, hundreds of thousands of Jewish refugees from Arab countries arrived in Israel in droves. The new Jewish immigrants who, in many cases, had been expelled from Jewish communities that had been established thousands of years ago in Arab lands, filled the vacuum left by the retreating Palestinians. None of these Jewish exiles received compensation for property they lost or were extended invitations to return to the Arab countries that had treated them brutally after the establishment of Israel as a state.

The Arab states that drove the Jews out of their lands, therefore, were in direct violation of **U.N. Resolution 194** which stated that *refugees wishing to return to their homes and live at peace with their neighbors should be permitted to do so...and compensation should be paid for loss or damage of property of those choosing not to return.* The Palestinians have referred to the same U.N. Resolution to claim their right to return to Israel. However, as revealed in the wording of the 1968 **PLO covenant** (which indirectly called for the destruction of Israel) and demonstrated by persistent militant activity, they have also instilled doubt that they would be willing to "live at peace with their neighbors."

Israelis have long feared that the goal of repatriation was to undermine the state of Israel and ultimately bring its destruction. Indeed, if Israel absorbed four million Palestinians to join the million Arab nationals currently living in the country, the Jewish state would cease to exist and Israel would become another Arab country in the Middle East.

---

[56] At the time, the inhabitants were simply considered "Arabs." The territorial distinction "Palestinian" was only later applied to the group.

[57] According to the Palestinians, the natives left for a variety of reasons including a perceived threat of ethnic cleansing, a desire to avoid the fighting between the Arabs and Israelis, fear of living among enemies and in response to orders by Israelis, Arabs and the British to evacuate. Israelis claim that in some cases, many Jews, including Ben-Gurion, urged the Arabs to remain and become full and equal citizens of Israel.

SETTLEMENTS

As stated in the **Torah** (and Bible), thousands of years ago God granted "all the land of Canaan" to **Abraham** and his descendants as an "everlasting possession." But when the Jews "defiled the House of Israel," and "polluted it with their idols," God became furious and scattered the Jews among many nations as punishment. [58]

Even in the **Diaspora** (the "dispersion"), though, Jews continued to turn in prayer toward the site of the holy Temple in Jerusalem where **Solomon** had housed the sacred **Ark of the Covenant** and yearned for the day when they could return to *Eretz-Israel* (the land of Israel).

In 1948, the Jews had their wish. As had been promised in the book of Ezekiel, (36:20-24), God had pity on the exiles and gathered the Jews from all the countries to bring them back to the land that he had given their forefathers.

Theologically, therefore, Jews believe that the land of **Canaan** (which includes the West Bank [Judea and Samaria] and Gaza) always belonged to them. With the re-creation of the state of Israel, Jews could finally return from Diaspora to join the Jewish communities that had remained and flourished in Jerusalem for thousands of years.

The Muslim Arab inhabitants, in contrast, never held the same intense sense of connection to this area. They revered the holy sites in Arabia (Mecca and Medina) above the Noble Sanctuary, Islam's third holiest site. Jerusalem had never been the capital city of a Muslim empire, and the inhabitants never considered themselves a separate state. The term "Palestinian," in fact, was a relatively recent distinction coined initially to distinguish this group from other Arabs and reinforce their claim to the land. Previously, the Arabs living in the area considered themselves members of the broader pan-Arab community.

Politically, Jews could trace their modern rights to the land from the 1917 **Balfour Declaration**, which demonstrated Britain's acceptance of a national home for the Jewish people in Palestine. The Declaration was reinforced by the League of Nations in the terms of the Mandate approved in 1922, which recognized the historical connection of the Jewish people with Palestine.

In 1947, the Arabs rejected the U.N. proposal to partition the land into Jewish and Arab sections and chose, instead, to settle the conflict over possession through war. As a result of armed combat, Jordan occupied and then annexed the West Bank (including eastern Jerusalem) and Egypt seized the Gaza Strip district.

For nearly two decades, the Jordanians prohibited Jews form visiting their most

---

[58] "When the house of Israel dwelt in their own land, they defiled it by their own way and by their doings...wherefore I poured my fury upon them for the blood that they had shed upon the land, and for their idols wherewith they had polluted it." [Ezekiel 36:17-18]

holy site, the **Temple Mount** in Jerusalem, until the West Bank was recaptured in 1967. In that year, Israel fought and won a defensive **Six-Day War** against the combined Arab forces of Syria, Egypt and Jordan and won control over the territories of Judea and Samaria (West Bank), the Gaza Strip and the Golan Heights.

Egypt never established sovereignty over the Gaza Strip and in 1988, Jordan relinquished all its claims to the West Bank. In the territorial vacuum, therefore, Israel became de facto administrators in the territories (rather than "occupiers" of land that belonged to another sovereign state) until permanent status was determined through peace agreements.

Since the territories were not technically "occupied," therefore, Israel's settlement in the West Bank and Gaza territories were not in violation of **Article 49 of the fourth Geneva Convention** (which stated that *occupying powers shall not deport or transfer parts of its own civilian population into the territory it occupies*) and Israelis were entitled to settle on land acquired in the 1967 war and enjoy governmental military protection. Denying the right of Jews to live in these territories, moreover, could be construed as racist in the same manner that barring Jews from living in New York, Paris or London would be deemed anti-Semitic.

The Jewish townships in Palestinian-occupied areas, moreover, were not built in violation of the **Oslo Accords** which did not contain provisions prohibiting the establishment or expansion of Jewish communities in the West Bank and Gaza.[59] Nor did they breach the 2002 **Road Map for Peace** which only obliged Israel to dismantle outposts and settlements once Palestinian attacks stopped (although some settlements were dismantled by Ariel Sharon as a good-will gesture despite the continued violence).

Lastly, the Israeli government did not establish settlements on private land that had been expropriated for this purpose. Settlements were only built on land that had been deemed "public" after exhaustive investigations confirmed that no individuals could claim private ownership to the land in question.

Critics
Jewish opponents of Israel's settlement policy have criticized that the outposts have become the greatest obstacle to peace and drain the government of valuable resources. The Israeli government spends more than $500 million a year on subsidies, infrastructure and education for the Jewish settlers living in the West Bank and Gaza -- not including the cost of military battalions dispatched to protect the neighborhoods.

The Israel advocacy group, **Peace Now**, has also complained that the outposts are illegal and breed hatred between the Israelis and the Palestinian people preventing any peaceful coexistence between the two groups.

---

[59] At Camp David, Menachem Begin agreed to put a three month moratorium on settlements in the West Bank. He kept his agreement.

JERUSALEM

One of the most contested pieces of real estate in the world, Jerusalem lies at the heart of the Israeli-Arab conflict. In the center of Jerusalem, the Temple Mount/Noble Sanctuary -- contiguous holy site to both the Muslims and the Jews -- remains the most bitter point of contention.

To the Muslims, the shrine on the **Noble Sanctuary** (considered the farthest or "al-aqsa" mosque) marks the spot where Mohammed ascended to heaven. After Mecca and Medina, the city is considered Islam's third holiest site.

According to Middle East historian Daniel Pipes, though, the importance of Jerusalem as a holy site was fabricated by Muslims for political reasons. The leaders of the **Umayyad Dynasty**, claims Pipes, sought to shift attention away from competing rulers in Arabia by enhancing the importance of its own territory. To accomplish this, the Umayyads interpreted the Quranic passage that stated that God took Mohammed "on a night journey from the sacred mosque in Mecca to the furthest (or al-aqsa) mosque" to mean that Mohammed had ascended to heaven from Jerusalem (the "furthest mosque"). Decades later, the Umayyads built the "Al-Aqsa" Mosque to mark the location.

Pipes further argued that the Muslims only embraced the holy city when it suited them politically, for example, after the conquest of Jerusalem by the Crusades (which was followed by the proliferation of literature extolling the virtues of the city), the acquisition by British troops and after the Israelis took Jerusalem in 1967.

The Jews, on the other hand, have always considered Jerusalem the uncontested "eternal capital" of Israel and an important part of Jewish identity. Since **King David** established Jerusalem as the capital of the Jewish state a thousand years before the Common Era (around 1000 B.C.) it has served as the cornerstone of Jewish life. Jews have prayed in the direction of the city since the **Babylonian Captivity** in the 6th century B.C. (see "Biblical History") and mourned the destruction of the Temple that had housed the sacred Ark of the Covenant carried by **Moses** across the Sinai desert. Greetings among Jews were punctuated with the hopeful phrase "next year in Jerusalem" and a vow to return to Jerusalem was written into Jewish prayer. No other group has so consistently cherished the sacred spirit of the city and no other state has made Jerusalem its capital. To designate any other city as Israel's capital, therefore, would go against the very foundation of Israel's identity.

Modern History of Jerusalem

Even before the Zionists began to settle in what was then Palestine, Jews made up the majority of the population in Jerusalem. By the time the British entered the city and made it the administrative center of the Mandate, Jews made up 70% of Jerusalem's inhabitants. But Jerusalem's contested status as capital to both the Jews and the Palestinians made the city a hotbed of conflict prompting the United Nations to propose internationalizing the city to keep the peace.

Israel in a Nutshell

The proposal, which was rejected by the Arabs, was nullified after Arab armies put the city under siege in 1948 and the city was divided for the first time in its history between the Jordanians and the Israelis.

Under **David Ben-Gurion** (Israel's first prime minister), the western portion of Jerusalem was made Israel's capital. The Jordanians, who had captured the eastern half of Jerusalem along with the West Bank, continued to rule from Jordan's capital in Amman and denied the Jewish people access to their holiest site, the **Western Wall** (the last remnant of Solomon's Temple). In the two decades of Jordanian rule, more than 50 synagogues were destroyed and thousands of Jewish residents were expelled from the territory.

The city was unified once again in 1967 after Israel's victory in the Six-Day War. Although Israeli rule now extended to the Temple Mount, Israel agreed in the interest of peace and tolerance to allow the Jordanian *waqf* (religious trust) to continue managing the site (the Israeli police would maintain control over security).

Currently, the Temple Mount is administered by the Palestinian *Mufti* (the head of the Muslim community in Jerusalem) appointed by PA president Yasser Arafat. Formally, the *waqf* administration is still answerable to the Jordanian government which pays employee salaries and operational expenses.

Resolution of the "Jerusalem issue" was only relegated to the "final stages" of the Oslo Treaties and the 2000 Camp David talks broke down over the inability of negotiators to compromise on the terms of sovereignty over the holy city.

In 2001, U.S. president **Bill Clinton** suggested the division of Jerusalem into pockets of Jewish and Palestinian control with the Temple Mount going to the Palestinian state and the Wailing Wall falling under Israeli sovereignty. The plan was rejected by both the Israelis, who bristled at the thought of turning over sovereignty of the Temple Mount to the Palestinians, and the Palestinians, who complained that the U.S. proposal broke up the area of Palestinian Jerusalem into tiny disconnected islands of control.

The issue of Jerusalem was again pushed to the final stage of the 2002 Road Map to Peace to be dealt with in Phase III scheduled to begin in 2004.

Enisen Publishing

*

Palestine
in a nutshell

The World in a Nutshell

Palestine in a Nutshell

* The Palestinian flag is composed of three bands -- from top to bottom: black, white, green -- with a red triangle pointing to the middle of the white band. The flag was originally designed by Sharif Hussein as the flag of Arab Revolt in June 1916. It was later recognized by the Arab League as the flag of the Palestinian people and officially adopted by the Palestinian National Council of the PLO in 1964.

The **red** portion represents the Hashemite family and was the flag of the Arab tribes who conquered North Africa and Andalusia (modern-day Spain). The Fatimid's (see "Ancient History") took **green** as their color to symbolize their allegiance to Ali, the Prophet Mohammed's cousin and son-in-law who wrapped himself in a green quilt to thwart an assassination attempt on the Prophet. The Umayyads adopted **white** as their emblematic color and the Abbasids were represented by a **black** flag symbolizing mourning for the murder of the Prophet's relatives. Early Muslims also went to battle carrying both a white flag dedicated to Allah and a black flag symbolizing revenge.

*****

Note: This book uses the initials B.C. ("before Christ") and A.D. ("Anno Domini" or "in the year of the Lord") rather than B.C.E. ("Before the Common Era") and C.E. (in the "Common Era") to designate years since the writer and editors felt these terms were most familiar to Nutshell Notes readers.

*****

We understand that future activities may modify or shed new light on some of the data in this book. For that reason, Nutshell Notes, L.L.C. and Enisen Publishing invite readers to visit our website www.nutshellnotes.com to learn about the latest developments concerning Israel/Palestine.

Special Thanks to:
Mike Chaplin and Avo Tavitian

Israel/Palestine
First edition - January 2004
First published - January 2004

Enisen Publishing
2118 Wilshire Boulevard, #351
Santa Monica, Ca 90403-5784
(866) ENISENP 866-364-7367
http://www.enisen.com
publishing@enisen.com
aroraback@msn.com

Text	Amanda Roraback
Maps	Katie Gerber
Cover design	C.W. Herlong
Editor-in-Chief	Dorothy Roraback
Asst. Editor	Paul Bernhard

ISBN #0-9702908-4-5
Printed in the United States of America

TABLE OF CONTENTS

ISRAEL/PALESTINE AT A GLANCE

The Region at a Glance

FACTS AND FIGURES

Name:	The Palestinian National Authority (PNA) is an autonomous national entity comprising the territories of Gaza (GZ) and the West Bank (WB)
Capital City:	Ramallah (Palestinian Authority Headquarters)
Area:	West Bank 3641 sq. mi. Gaza Strip 224 sq. mi.
Government:	Palestinian Authority (created May 1994)
Head of Government:	President Yasser Arafat (July 1994 -)
Chief of State:	Prime Minister Ahmed Korei (Oct. 7, 2003 -)
Population:	2,237,194 (WB), 1,274,868 (GZ)
Age structure:	0-14 years 44.1% (WB) 49.4% (GZ) , 15-64 years: 52.4% (WB), 47.9% (GZ), 65 years and over: 3.5% (WB), 2.7% (GZ) median age, tot. 17.9% (WB), 15.3 (GZ)
Population growth rate:	3.3% (WB), 3.89% (GZ)
Total fertility rate:	4.65 children born per woman (WB) 6.17 children born per woman (GZ)
Ethnic groups:	Palestinian Arab 83%, Jewish 17% (WB) Palestinian Arab 99.4%, Jewish 0.6% (GZ)
Religions:	(WB) Muslim 75% (predominantly Sunni), Jewish 17%, Christian and other 8%
	(GZ) Muslim 98.7% (predominantly Sunni), Christian 0.7%, Jewish 0.6%
Languages:	Arabic, Hebrew (spoken by Israeli settlers and many Palestinians), English (widely understood)
GDP (per capita):	$800 (WB), $600 (GZ)
Pop. below the poverty line:	60% (WB and GZ) (2002 est.)
Unemployment rate:	50%
Telephones:	95,729 (total for West Bank and Gaza Strip)
Airports:	3 (WB), 2 (GZ)
Military branches:	In accordance with the peace agreement, the Palestinian Authority is not permitted conventional military forces; there is, however, a Public Security Force and a civil Police Force.
Military manpower:	Police and Security Forces: 29,000 (2002)

Figures taken from the CIA World Factbook 2003

TERMS

Yasser Arafat (full name: Mohammed Abdul-Ra'ouf Arafat as Qudwa al-Husseini, also known in the Arab world by his nom-de-guerre, **Abu Ammar)**
Leader of the Fatah party since 1958, chairman of the PLO since 1969 and president of the Palestinian Authority since 1996.

PLO - Palestine Liberation Organization
The PLO was formed and sponsored by the Arab League in 1964 as an umbrella organization for Palestinian liberation movements. In 1969, the PLO was taken over by Fatah, an underground network of secret cells advocating armed struggle against Israel, and came under Palestinian control. Yasser Arafat, one of Fatah's founders, was elected chairman of the PLO in the same year. In 1974, the Arab League recognized the PLO as the "sole legitimate representative of the Palestinian people,"

Palestinian (National) Authority (PA or PNA)
The PNA was established under the terms of the Oslo Accords as an autonomous national entity comprising Gaza and the West Bank. In January 1996, Yasser Arafat was elected the Authority's first president and 88 others were elected to sit on a Palestinian Legislative Council. The position of prime minister was created in March 2003.

Mahmoud Abbas (Abu Mazen)
Abbas served as the Palestinian Authority's first prime minister from March 2003 until his resignation on September 6, 2003. He was replaced by **Ahmed Korei** (also called Abu Alaa). Both Abbas and Korei participated in the Oslo peace negotiations in 1993. Korei, who was also involved in he peace talks at Camp David in July 2000 (see "peace treaties" in Israel section), is believed to have been named a possible successor to Arafat in case of death or injury until a new election is organized.

Rejectionists
Rejectionists are members of a radical segment of the Palestinian national movement who continue to reject the Oslo-based peace process, the legitimacy of the state of Israel and, in some cases, the validity of the Palestinian Authority. Among the rejectionist factions are the Palestinian Islamic Jihad, PFLP-GC (see "PFLP"), and the Al-Aqsa Martyr's Brigade. Through armed struggle, the rejectionists hope to derail the peace process and establish a Palestinian state in all of historic Palestine.

Greater Syria
The region that historically included the present-day states of Jordan, Israel, Lebanon and Syria.

Intifada
Literally meaning "shaking off" in Arabic, the term has been applied to the Palestinian uprising that began in 1987 and reignited in 2000 after the visit to the Haram al- Sharif (Noble Sanctuary) by Israel's then-Defense Minister Ariel Sharon.

Arab

One who speaks Arabic (originally natives of Arabia). Although most Arabs are Muslim, Arabs can also be Christian or Jewish. Persians from Iran (who speak Farsi), Turks (who speak Turkish), Pakistanis, Afghans etc. are not ethnically Arab.

Palestinian

A person who comes from Palestine, the region on the east coast of the Mediterranean west of the Jordan River. The word comes from the "Philistines," the ancient Sea People who resided in Canaan about 1200 B.C. Most Palestinians are Arab Muslims but can also follow other faiths.

Muslim

One who observes the Islamic faith.

Jihad

Arabic word meaning "struggle" or "striving" denoting the Muslim obligation to struggle against one's own vices or against those things that threaten the Islamic faith. The word is often translated simply as a "holy war."

Haram al-Sharif

Also known as the Noble Sanctuary and called the Temple Mount by the Jews, Muslims believe that the Prophet Mohammed was transported to the site in a "night journey" that brought him from the nearest mosque (in Mecca) to the furthest or "al-Aqsa" mosque in Jerusalem.

Dome of the Rock

Structure built upon the Noble Sanctuary over the spot from which Mohammed ascended to Heaven.

Al-Aqsa Mosque

Mosque built on the Noble Sanctuary in Jerusalem to commemorate Mohammed's night journey to paradise.

Separation Wall'

Dubbed the "Apartheid Wall" or "Berlin Wall" by its detractors, construction on the barrier wall/fence built by Israelis roughly along the *green line* borders between Israeli and the Palestinian territories began in 2003 and is expected to extend more than 403 miles upon its completion.

Hizbollah (also Hezbollah and Hizb allah, "party of Allah")

Iranian-backed Islamic struggle movement based in Lebanon. the organization is an umbrella organization of various radical Shi'ite groups inspired by the Islamic Revolution in Iran and adhering to the ideology of the revolution's leader, the late Ayatollah Khomeini. Hizbollah was established in 1982 in Lebanon after the Israeli invasion and occupation of Beirut and is committed to the struggle against the Zionist enemy in Israel and "western imperialism" in general. It is also committed to the establishment of an Islamic republic in Lebanon. The group's members especially object to the presence of Israeli Defense Forces (IDF) in Lebanon.

Palestine in a Nutshell

ANCIENT HISTORY

Before it was called Palestine or Israel or even Syria and Lebanon, the land between Jordan and the Mediterranean Sea was known as Canaan and its inhabitants, **Canaanites**.

The Canaanites, who had established themselves in the area around the 4th millennium B.C., were a Semitic-people (so-called because they spoke a language supposedly shared by descendants of **Shem**, Noah's oldest son -- Hebrew, Aramaic and Arabic are all Semitic languages). The Canaanites settled in a number of city-states including one of the world's oldest known towns, Jericho. Around 3000 B.C., one of the Canaanite tribes, the **Jebusites**, built a settlement which they called Ur-Salem, the "city of peace" or Jerusalem.[1]

For much of its history, Canaan was dominated politically by the Egyptians who were able to repel incursions by Amorites, Hittites and Hurrians. But by the 13th century, Egyptian power began to weaken allowing the land to be invaded by armed bands of Philistines and a confederation of Hebrew-speaking tribes.

In spite of the invasions, some of the inland Canaanites, like the **Jebusites** of Jerusalem, remained in the interior of the land. Most of the Canaanites, however, fled to a narrow strip of coastal land in the north – a region that was subsequently known as Phoenicia (in modern-day Lebanon). The **"Phoenicians"** (the name given to coastal Canaanites by the Greeks) became sea-faring traders and colonized a number of new cities -- Tyre (which the Phoenicians called Al-Sur).[2] Sidon, Beirut, Byblos and Ugarit. In order to make it easier to keep merchant records, the Phoenicians simplified the 55-character cuneiform style of writing that had been developed in Mesopotamia in the 4th millennium B.C., into 22 distinct sounds. After alterations by the Greeks and Romans, this "phonetic"[3] alphabet became the precursor to our current 26-letter alphabet.

The **Philistines**, who invaded the southern coastal plain of Canaan in about 1200 B.C., were Sea People[4] of Aegean and southeastern European origin. With their iron weaponry and military skills, they swiftly conquered the Hittite Empire, Cyprus, Mycenae (the most powerful of the ancient Greek kingdoms) and almost defeated Egypt before they settled in Canaan. In their new home, they established five kingdoms: Gaza, Ashkelon, Ashdod, Gath and Ekron collectively known as "Philistia" or "Palestine" by Herodotus and other Greek and Latin writers.

At about the same time, another group of people from Egypt called the **Israelites** (or Hebrews) arrived in Palestine. In 1230 B.C., the Israelites, led by

---

1 Also called Urusalim, Ur-Shalem or the "house of Salem," (Salem was the chieftain of the clan of the Jebusites.)

2 From where the name "Syria" derived.

3 The words "phonetic," "phonics" and "phone" (sharing the root *phone* meaning "voice" or "sound") all come from the "Phoenicians" and their alphabet. Furthermore, the invention of the alphabet took place in the city of Byblos which was famous for its trade in papyrus (ancient "paper"). The Greek word *biblio* or "book" comes from "Byblos" as do the words "Bible" and "bibliography" in English.

4 The Sea Peoples were made up of an alliance of five groups with the Pelesets (Philistines) the most powerful among them.

Joshua, conquered the Canaanites and settled in the hill country in the interior of the land. But they could not defeat the superior military organization of the Philistines (symbolized in the Bible as the mighty giant Goliath). After a particularly devastating defeat in Shiloh in 1050 B.C. (during which the Philistines took the Ark of the Covenant, the Israelites most sacred object), the twelve Hebrew tribes decided to unite under an appointed king, Saul. According to Jewish legend, a young boy named **David** decided to challenge the Philistine giant, **Goliath**, who was protected by a "helmet of bronze and a coat of chain mail." With a single stone hurled from a slingshot, David hit Goliath's forehead, the only vulnerable spot in Goliath's armor, causing the giant to tumble to the ground.[5] The boy became the Israelites greatest king.

Under David's command, the Israelites ultimately defeated the Philistines in 1000 B.C.. Soon after the conquest, King David captured the city of Jerusalem (then called the City of David) and made it his capital. On the site of Mount Moriah to the north of the city, David's son, **Solomon**, built a temple to house the Ark of the Covenant which contained the tablets of the Ten Commandments.

Under Solomon's rule, the empire's influence stretched from the Gulf of Aqaba to the Euphrates River. But the united kingdom could not survive Solomon's death. In 922 B.C., the country of the Israelites was divided into a northern Kingdom of Israel composed of ten of the twelve Hebrew tribes and a southern Kingdom of Judah which controlled Jerusalem. The ten tribes in the north were scattered among distant lands when the kingdom was conquered by the Assyrians in 722 B.C.. **Judah** survived until the **Babylonians**[6] under king **Nebuchadnezzar** invaded the territory in 586 B.C..

In order to solidify his authority in Palestine, Babylonian king Nebuchadnezzar deported the most influential Jews (priests, professionals, craftsmen, the wealthy etc.) to his capital of Babylon where they continued to practice their religion. He then burned Solomon's temple to the ground and ravaged the city of Jerusalem. The Philistines, who had lost their preeminent position in the territory after the establishment of Israel and Judah, assimilated into the Assyrian and Babylonian cultures.

When the Persians under **Cyrus the Great** overthrew the Babylonians in 538 B.C., the Jews were allowed to return to Judah. Influenced by the belief preached by Zarathustra (Zoroaster in Greek) in the 7th century B.C. that the universe was divided into spheres of good an evil, Cyrus was anxious to ally himself with the "good" god of the Jews, **Yahweh**. Good and evil, it was prophesied would soon fight in a cosmic battle and Cyrus believed that his Persian Empire could help bring about the triumph of good over evil. The Jews were instructed to rebuild their Temple and Judah became a theological state where only the worship of the Jewish god was permitted and adherence to Hebrew law was encouraged.

---

5 While the story of the underdog vs. the well-armed giant has been used to illustrate the spiritual might of the monotheistic Israelites over their pagan enemies, the metaphor could also be applied today to describe the battle between the young unarmed Palestinian "Davids" trying to defeat the gun-toting Israeli "Goliaths" with sticks and stones.
6 The "New" Babylonians are also called the Chaldeans.

GRECO-ROMAN PERIOD

For 200 years the Jews were allowed to practice their religion freely in Judah under Persian rule. The Greeks, who conquered the Persians in 332 B.C. and made Palestine a Greek state a year later, also admired the Jewish religious traditions and allowed the citizens of Judah to exercise political autonomy. The **Torah**, the Hebrews' holy book, was translated into Greek (facilitating the spread of the Jewish concepts of God, Mosaic law etc.) and the Jews were permitted to settle in other parts of the empire as Greek citizens.

But the infusion of Hellenistic (Greek) culture, while appealing in some ways to Hebrew scholars because of its emphasis on reason, logic and dialogue, began to challenge the Jewish tradition. As control of Palestine passed from **Alexander the Great**'s successor **Ptolemy** to **Seleucus** in 198 B.C., the new leaders abandoned Alexander's policy of tolerance and attempted to force Hellenism upon the population. The drastic Hellenizing measures of Seleucid emperor **Antiochus IV Epiphanes** (175-163 B.C.) -- altering Jewish scriptures, engaging priests in wrestling contests in Greek fashion, desecrating the temple etc. -- instigated a Jewish rebellion led by **Judas Maccabee**. For nearly 100 years after this successful rebellion, the Jews enjoyed political independence until the Roman invasion by **Pompey the Great** in 63 B.C..

Under the Romans the province of Judea (the Latin name for Judah) was placed under the command of a Jewish family, the Herods, who had gained favor with the Romans. It was under the reign of **King Herod** (the greatest of the Herodian kings) from 37-4 B.C., that Jerusalem began to expand and the prophet **Jesus of Nazareth** was born. Herod ordered the construction of new cities, aqueducts, fortresses, stadiums and, most notably, enlarged and enhanced the Temple in Jerusalem. But although Herod and his family practiced Jewish law (following dietary codes, not allowing women in the family to marry uncircumcised men etc.), his allegiance to the Romans alienated him from the Jewish community.[7]

According to the Bible, Herod, the self-proclaimed "King of the Jews," was particularly incensed when he learned that another "king of the Jews" was going to be born in Bethlehem. To prevent the potential usurper from taking the throne from his sons, Herod ordered the slaughter of all boys under the age of two living in the city.

To escape the decree, Mary and Joseph[8] took their newborn son, Jesus, to Egypt. The prophet (called Christ, the "anointed one," by his followers) returned to Palestine years later to preach monotheism in Galilee and attracted many followers. His message and influence, though, conflicted with that of the Jewish and Roman authority and he was sentenced to death by crucifixion

---

[7] The Jews were insulted, for instance, when Herod placed an eagle, the Roman emblem, atop the Temple. Herod executed the Jews who tore it down.

[8] The Muslims believe that Jesus was miraculously conceived without a father, but at that time, was derided by the locals as an illegitimate child.

around A.D. 29.

According to Muslim tradition the prophet Jesus was not killed but was raised instead to heaven by God[9] to save him from his adversaries. Meanwhile the Jews who hadn't acknowledged Jesus as God's messenger were condemned by God to suffer under Roman oppression.

Roman tyranny over the Jews intensified at the beginning of the 1st century finally provoking the Jews to revolt in A.D. 70. But the rebellion was crushed and, in revenge, the Romans laid siege to Jerusalem and destroyed Herod's temple.[10] A second uprising in A.D. 132 was also brutally suppressed, this time ending with the execution and enslavement of large numbers of Jews and the banishment of others. Christianity was outlawed and Jews, from that time on, were forbidden to enter Jerusalem (which had been renamed Aelia Capitolina by the new **Emperor Hadrian** and dedicated to the Roman god Zeus). The city lost its religious, economic and political significance until Christianity was legalized by **Emperor Constantine** in A.D. 313.

Under Constantine, a new interest in Jesus' life inspired Christian pilgrims to visit holy sites in Jerusalem and monuments and churches were erected at the most momentous locations: the place where Jesus had ceremoniously performed the sacraments of the Last Supper, for example, next to the spot where Jesus had reportedly risen from the dead, the location of Jesus' crucifixion (designated by the Church of the Holy Sepulchre) etc.

Jerusalem's status as a holy city to the Jews and, under Constantine, to the Christians was further enhanced three centuries later with the rise of Islam.

---

[9] The Quran says "They [the Jews] denied the truth and uttered a monstrous falsehood against Mary. [The Jews] said in boast 'we killed Christ Jesus' but they killed him not nor crucified him but so it was made to appear to them...nay Allah [God] raised him up unto Himself..." Quran 4:157.

[10] Only one wall of Herod's Temple, called the Western or "Wailing Wall" by the Jews, remains to this day.

ISLAM

The Story of Abraham

Abraham, Muslims claim, was the patriarch of the Jews, the Christians and the Muslims and the holy books of all three religions agree about most of his history. However, the **Torah** (or Old Testament to the Christians) and the Islam's holy books (the **Quran** and the **Hadiths**) differ in the details.

While the *Torah* includes little about Abraham's youth in the city of Ur (in present-day Iraq), the *Quran* and *Hadiths* (stories collected by Mohammed's followers) illustrate Abraham's conflicts with the polytheistic idolaters.

According to the *Hadiths*, Abraham was born to a father who produced sculptures of idols for the Mesopotamian pagans. As a child, Abraham would play with the idols as if they were toys and laughed when he saw his people worshipping the statues as if they were gods.

One day, he decided to prove to the idolaters that these stones had no supernatural power by destroying all but the largest one while the people were enjoying a feast on the riverbank. When the worshippers returned to find their idols shattered, he told them that the biggest idol was responsible for the destruction and that they should ask the statue themselves if they did not believe him. When the people admitted that idols could not speak or move, Abraham took the opportunity to demonstrate how foolish the idolaters had been to worship lifeless objects. But the angry crowds were offended by his allegation and called for Abraham to be thrown into a large fire. Abraham's life was spared when God cooled the fire.

Namrud, the King of Babylon who had proclaimed himself a god, was also threatened by Abraham's claims that his god was the one and only God -- a deity more powerful than the gods recognized by the idolaters and far greater than any earthly king. "My Lord, Allah, makes the sun rise from the East." Abraham challenged the Babylonian king, "Can you make it rise from the West?" The hostility generated by Abraham's unorthodox views finally led to the prophets departure.

In the book of *Genesis* (the first book of the Christian *Bible* and Jewish Torah), the Lord told Abraham to leave the country "unto a land that I will show thee."

Muslims, instead, claim it was Abraham's decision to leave Mesopotamia with two followers, a man named Lot (who settled in Sodom) and Abraham's wife **Sarah**, to spread his message of monotheism elsewhere. Abraham helped the poor and performed other good deeds in the course of his travels that took him from Ur to Palestine and then to Egypt -- where Sarah was given a servant called **Hagar** by the Egyptian king.

Both the *Bible* and the *Quran* agree that Sarah was old and barren and that she offered Abraham her Egyptian servant, Hagar, to bear him children.

The *Bible* tells us that once Hagar successfully conceived Abraham's child, a child called **Ishmael**, Sarah became so angry that Hagar was forced to flee from her wrath. The Lord found the frightened Hagar by a fountain of water in the wilderness and told her to return to her mistress. For her obedience, God promised to "multiply her seed" and assured her that her son would "beget princes

who would make a great nation."

After Ishmael's birth, the Muslims say that Abraham was instructed by God to take Hagar and and her baby to an empty, uncultivated valley in the Arabian Peninsula and leave her there with only enough food and water for two days. In anguish, Abraham cried "O Lord, I have made some of my offspring to dwell in a valley with no cultivation by your Sacred House (the site of a meteor [the Ka'aba] in Mecca believed to have spiritual powers) in order that they may offer prayers perfectly. So fill some hearts among men with love towards them and provide them with fruits so that they may give thanks."

When the water ran out, Hagar ran back and forth in a panic until she saw an angel at the place of Zam Zam digging into the earth until water flowed. Later, some people from the tribe of Jurhum saw a bird flying around the new water source and joined Hagar and her child at the well. The people decided to settle there with Hagar and sent for their families who came and became permanent residents (the ancestors of the Arabs). Ishmael grew up and learned Arabic from the settlers who admired him for his virtues.

Some years later, Abraham returned to visit his son and the two built a sacred house (the **Ka'aba**) to give the people a place where they could pray to **Allah** (God). The structure (in Mecca, Saudi Arabia) remains Islam's holiest site.

According to Jews and Christians, as a reward to Abraham for observing his promise that he and all the men in his household be circumcised, his wife Sarah, miraculously became pregnant herself at the age of 99 with a child who would be called **Isaac**. The book of *Genesis* tells us that God instructed Abraham to take his beloved son, Isaac, to the region of Moriah (the site of the Temple Mount) and sacrifice him there as an offering.

Muslims claim that it was, in fact, Hagar's son, **Ishmael**, that Abraham nearly sacrificed in Mecca, not Moriah, and only after a dream that the prophet had interpreted as God's instruction.

"O my son!" lamented Abraham to Ishmael, "I have seen in a dream that I am slaughtering you, what do you think?" "O my father," replied Ishmael, "Do that which you are commanded if God wills it and you will find me patient." Once they had both submitted themselves to the will of God and Ishmael had laid himself down to be killed, Allah said "Abraham, you have fulfilled the dream" then sent down a big sheep from heaven to be slaughtered in place of Abraham's son. The event is celebrated by Muslims today as the **Festival of Sacrifice** (or *Eid al-Adha*) with prayers, feasting and the exchanging of gifts.

Abraham, Muslims claim, apart from being the first to practice monotheism and the ancestor of three great religions, was also the first person to use the word *Islam* or "submission" when referring to a believer's relationship to God. Those who submit to the will of god (as Abraham had done in compliance with God's order to sacrifice Ishmael), are called "Muslims."

Birth of Islam

Thousands of years after Abraham and his son Ishmael dedicated the Ka'aba in Mecca to the worship of God, his descendants reverted to idol worship, a practice that Abraham had denounced in his hometown of Ur. Arab pilgrims still

considered the Ka'aba a holy site but by the 6th century A.D. the structure had been filled with sculptures representing a pantheon of false gods. In this environment, a new prophet called **Mohammed** was born.

Mohammed was born in Mecca in A.D. 570 to the **Quraish** clan which ruled the city at the time. Mohammed was orphaned at a young age and lived with his beloved uncle **Abu Talib**. In his youth, he had accompanied his uncle on a commercial trip to Syria where he met a Christian monk who prophesied that Mohammed would play a noble role in the future.

When he was 25, Mohammed married a wealthy widow named **Khadija** and lived a relatively tranquil life helping her run a caravan business she had inherited from her late husband.

As Mohammed approached the age of 40, he became more and more introspective and often retreated to a cave near Mecca to pray and meditate. During one of his sessions an angel appeared to tell him that he had been chosen to be a messenger of God sent to lead the fallen people back to the knowledge and service of Allah (God). The revelation was the first in a series of oracles he would receive in his lifetime that would eventually be compiled into Islam's holy book, the **Quran**.

In time, Mohammed (now called a "Prophet") attracted followers -- many from the lower and less privileged Arab classes who were drawn by his teachings that all men were equal. But polytheism was deeply rooted and the ruling classes, whose welfare and prestige depended on the sacred status of the idols in the Ka'aba and the resulting pilgrimage business, were wary of any challenge to their authority. In order to lessen the Prophets influence, the Quraish tribal leaders tried to convince people that Mohammed was just a dangerous magician with heretical ideas and harassed those who believed in his divine nature.

When the persecution became too great, Mohammed and his followers decided to seek refuge in **Yathrib** (later called **Medina**), a city to the north of Mecca populated in part by Muslim converts from the Jewish tribe of Khazraj.

Mohammed's Night Journey to the Al-Aqsa Mosque
In A.D. 619, the Prophet Mohammed made a "night journey" while he slept from the Al Masjid al Haram Mosque (the "nearest" mosque in Mecca) to the farthest or "al-aqsa" mosque believed to be the site of the Temple Mount in Jerusalem. Mohammed recalled that while in the holy city his soul was cleansed and filled with belief before the angel **Gabriel** accompanied him on a journey through the seven heavens. In the nearest heaven, Mohammed reported, he saw Adam, the first man. In the second heaven, the Prophet met with John the Baptist and Jesus who both greeted him warmly. As he rose through the next levels of heaven, Mohammed came into contact with the prophets Joseph, Enoch and Aaron. In the 6th heaven, Mohammed was greeted by Moses who wept "after me there has been sent a young man whose followers will enter Paradise in greater numbers than my followers." Finally, in the seventh heaven, Mohammed met Abraham and from there, the Prophet was taken to "the Lote Tree of the utmost boundary" where God advised him and his followers to engage in prayers five times a day.

Medina and the Jews

After Mohammed and his followers settled in Yathrib in A.D. 622, (the migration is called the *hijrah* in Arabic) the city changed its name to Medina, the "Illuminated City." At the time, Medina was inhabited by three distinct groups: the Emigrants (Muslims from Mecca and converts), Helpers (those who were friendly to Muslims but maintained idolatrous tendencies) and those who practiced Judaism.

Initially, Mohammed had developed a kinship with the Jews and hoped that they would receive him as their Messiah.[11] After his "night journey," in fact, Mohammed had instructed his followers to pray towards Jerusalem (the same direction the Jews faced to pray) and to follow many of the same rituals (dietary restrictions, fasting, circumcision, alms-giving etc.). But the Jews rejected his claim and Mohammed, in turn, renounced them.

As the relationship between the Jews and the Prophet disintegrated, religious practices were altered to distinguish Mohammed's followers from their rivals. The Sabbath, or day of rest, was changed from Saturday to Friday, for example, fasting rules were changed and the people were instructed to pray towards Mecca rather than Jerusalem.

Return to Mecca

In the second year of the *hijrah* the idolaters in Mecca began a series of hostile acts against the Muslims of Medina compelling the Prophet to organize his people into a military force. In the first incursion, the small band of Muslims was able to drive back the Meccan infidel armies leading the Muslims to feel secure in the belief that Allah and the angels were behind them.

Six years after the Prophet and his followers had arrived in Medina, the Muslims were eager to return to their birthplace. The Prophet, at first, had made a treaty with the Meccans to allow his people to peacefully make a pilgrimage to the Sacred House of the Ka'aba. The next year, however, the infidels attacked one of tribes allied with the Muslims, thereby breaking the treaty and compelling Mohammed's now substantial army to take measures.

The Muslim army entered the city of Mecca quietly and peacefully: no man was harmed; no house was robbed. The only command was to destroy the idols and pagan images. Like Abraham, thousands of years earlier, Mohammed entered the Ka'aba and smashed all 350 idols and rededicated the sacred house to God.

After this, great multitudes of people came to adopt the Islamic faith and take the oath of allegiance to the Prophet. The people vowed not to revere any deity but God, to obey the Prophet and to abstain from theft, adultery, infanticide and lying. Disciples were sent in every direction to preach Islam among the tribes of the deserts until nearly all the tribes of Arabia had submitted to the beliefs of the Prophet and sent emissaries to pay him homage.

---

[11] Jews believed a redeemer and savior would be sent by God who would bring together their outcasts and strengthen their obedience to the Divine precepts. "For then will I turn to the people a pure language, that all may call by the name of God and serve him unanimously. (Zeph. 3:9).

Thus, the mission of the Prophet had been accomplished, idolatry had been destroyed and the once cruel, superstitious and warring people were now united in a single charitable faith. In February A.D.632 Mohammed performed his last pilgrimage to Mecca and later that year the Prophet died.

The Spread of Islam

Mohammed had left no instructions as to who should follow him as the leader of the Muslim world after his death. The prime contenders were the Prophet's cousin **Ali**, whom Mohammed had adopted as his son, the Prophet's faithful friend and father-in-law, **Abu Bakr**, and one of his companions **Umar** (or **Omar) ibn Abd al-Khattab**. After much debate, the leaders of the Muslim community chose Abu Bakr to be Mohammed's successor or *caliph*.

Bakr's first duty was to reassert Muslim authority over the Bedouin Arab tribes whose oaths of allegiance to Mohammed threatened to crumble after the Prophets death. In order to consolidate the Arabian tribes, an army led by **Khalid** (a member of the Quraish tribe who had converted to Islam) was created. These forces began to push the Muslim Empire beyond the Arabian Peninsula into adjacent lands. The Mesopotamians across the Euphrates River, weakened by battles between the Byzantines in the West and the Sassanid Persians in the East, were the first to fall under Muslim might. Bakr then instigated the expansion of Islam into the Byzantine Empire (which at that time included Syria, Palestine and Egypt). In July 634, the Muslims under Khalid decisively defeated the Romans in Syria.

Bakr, already an old man when he was elected the first *caliph*, died a month after the battle and was replaced right away by **Umar,** a strong-minded military genius, who continued the expansion of the Muslim state. Under the title of "Commander of the Faithful," Umar marched into Palestine, Egypt and the Persian Empire with little resistance from the inhabitants. The Muslims' unique policy of tolerance appealed to the populace that had been suffering from conflicts among the different religious groups vying for ultimate authority.

When Umar received word that Jerusalem was ready to give in to the new religious warriors in 638, he entered the city himself to accept the surrender. Once in the Holy City, Umar proceeded to search for the rock on which Mohammed had prayed during his "night journey" and ordered that no prayers be made at the spot until the area was cleansed by three rainfalls.

After hearing of the bloodless occupation of Damascus two years earlier and Umar's humble entry into the city (he reportedly rode into Jerusalem wearing simple clothes and accompanied only by a single servant) the people were relieved. Upon his arrival, Umar assured the inhabitants that their lives would be safe and that they would have complete security for their property and their churches. As had been promised in Damascus, he also promised the people of Jerusalem that nothing but good would befall them as long as they paid the poll tax (*jizya*) and obeyed the laws.

Jews and Christians, as "People of the Book," were accorded a special status under the Muslim empire as *dhimmies*. *Dhimmies* were allowed to freely practice their own faiths and manage their own communities but were prohibited from bearing arms, serving in public office or building religious structures taller

than Muslim mosques.

Although Islam wasn't forced on the people, conversions did take place voluntarily on a mass scale for a number of reasons: Islam's recognition of Jewish and Christian prophets (Abraham, Moses, Jesus etc.) made the new faith more accessible; Muslims were exempted from paying the poll tax; conversion simply required a proclamation that Allah [God] was the only god and that Mohammed was his last Prophet; and all Muslims were considered equal under God (an appealing concept to impoverished and underprivileged converts).

Along with the spread of Islam, the arrival of the Arab armies to the area introduced the Arabic language which quickly replaced Aramaic and Coptic as the common language.

In order to govern the vast new territory consisting of Syria (including Palestine), Mesopotamia, Persia and Egypt (which was taken from the Byzantines in 642),[12] Umar divided the conquered countries into provinces and appointed governors from the powerful Umayyad family to manage the land.

Umar also established a public treasury, a police department, a judicial system that was separate form the executive branch of government, built schools and instituted governmental distribution of stipends to poor Jews and Christians (one of the five pillars of Islam requires Muslims to pay alms).

When Umar was killed in 644 by a Persian slave,[13] the pious **Uthman** (or **Othman**) **ibn Affan** from the Umayyad clan was elected the third *caliph* despite objections from believers who thought that **Ali**, Mohammed's cousin and son-in-law, was the Prophet's rightful successor. The division between Muslims who believed only the Prophet's blood relatives could follow him (the **Shi'ites**) and those who believed that the Muslim community should be led by elected leaders (the **Sunni**) eventually caused a schism that split the empire in two.

Uthman incorporated a number of new territories into the Islamic domain including Armenia, Caucasia, Cyprus and much of North Africa. Uthman was also responsible for establishing an official version of the **Quran** (Islam's holy book). But the *caliph* was a weak and unpopular ruler whose government was sullied by corruption and nepotism. Uthman, like his predecessor, was assassinated in 656 by a group of mutineers from Egypt.

To the satisfaction of the Shi'ites, Uthman's death finally brought the appointment of Ali as the Muslim Community's fourth *caliph*. One of the new *caliph*'s first calls of action was to clean up the corrupt administration that he had inherited from his predecessor by ordering all the worst offending governors to step down. But one of these governors, the governor of Syria and Uthman's nephew, **Mu'awiya**, refused to vacate his post opting, instead, to lead an insurrection against Ali.

In a scene of intrigue and conspiracy following Mu'awiya's bid for the Caliphate and calls for vengeance against Uthman's killers, plots were devised to murder both the governor and the *caliph*. While Mu'awiya escaped his death sentence,

---

[12] The imperial rule of Persians and Byzantines was very unpopular in the provinces. The Arab invasion, therefore, was welcomed by most of the population.

[13] Umar's assassin was a Shi'ite who, like other Shi'ites, believed that Ali should have been Mohammed's successor.

Ali did not. He was assassinated in the city of Najaf (in present-day Iraq).

With Ali out of the way, Mu'awiya claimed control over the Muslim Empire in 661 as the sixth *caliph* ushering in the **Umayyad Dynasty** and moving the capital of the Empire from Medina to Damascus, Syria. With the center of the empire shifted to the Levant,[14] incursions to the West through the Mediterranean Sea were much easier to accomplish. The empire was thus expanded to North Africa and Spain and Arabic was declared the state language in all the conquered areas.

The Muslims pushed their way as far as the Pyrenees Mountains on the border with France with the help of Berbers from North Africa. In the newly conquered territory, the **Moors** (Muslims of mixed Arab and Berber descent) established some of the most civilized and advanced cities in Europe. The Spanish Jews (**Sephardim**), who had welcomed the Muslims as liberators from the **Visigoths**, enjoyed a Golden Age of development under Moorish rule over al-Andalus (Spain).

Jerusalem under the Umayyads became a very important political and religious center and many impressive palaces were built in the city at this time. In an effort to change the character of the city from Christian Byzantine to Muslim, the Ummayads restored the walls of the ancient Temple of Solomon and built two mosques on the site of the **Noble Sanctuary** (or *Haram al-Sharif*[15]) to commemorate Mohammed's "night journey" to the seven heavens. The **Dome of the Rock** (the structure built to protect the stone from which Mohammed is said to have been lifted to heaven[16]) and the **al-Aqsa Mosque** attracted pilgrims from all over the Muslim world.

Central power shifted away from Jerusalem in 770, however, when the rebellious **Abbasids** (a coalition of Arabs rallied behind the descendants the Prophet's uncle, al-Abbas) took power from the Umayyads[17] and moved the capital of the Muslim empire to the Persian city of Baghdad.[18]

The more religious and cosmopolitan Abbasids launched Islam's Golden Age from their Persian capital of Baghad which became the most impressive city in the world (sometimes called "the Paris of the ninth century"). The city was filled with magnificent gardens, mosques and palaces that underscored the esteemed role of the *caliphs* who now considered themselves not only the successor to the Prophet but deputies of Allah himself.

Under the Dynasty's greatest *caliphs* **Harun al-Rashid** (famous because of his portrayal in the novel "A Thousand and One Nights") and his son **al-Mamun**,

---

14 The Levant is the name for the region on the Eastern coast of the Mediterranean Sea including present-day Lebanon, Syria, Palestine, Egypt, Greece and all the countries in between.

15 Known as the Temple Mount to the Jews.

16 To Jews this is the site where Isaac was prepared to be slaughtered as a sacrifice by Abraham.

17 The Umayyad Dynasty had been weakening because of financial crises (as the conversion rate to Islam grew, the revenue from the tax-paying non-Muslim population shrank) and feuding among the Arab groups (between Shi'ites and Sunnis, religious conservatives and liberals, the aristocracy and the ruling classes etc.).

18 One of the Umayyad princes fled to Spain where he established three centuries of Umayyad rule over al-Andalus (Spain) with the capital in Cordoba.

great strides were made in mathematics, astronomy, chemistry, technology, medicine, literature and the Muslim religion. The mathematical system of algebra was developed at this time as were Arabic numerals (including a symbol for zero), and pharmaceutical remedies that are still used today. The Abbasids were also responsible for compiling a vast collection of *hadiths* (accounts of the Prophet's life) that brought greater clarity and interest in the Muslim religion.

But the empire began to decline after the appointment of Mamun's son as *caliph*. Provinces began to fall into the hands of independent dynasties and rebellions by Persian peasants, African slaves and other groups destabilized the central authority.

By the mid 9th century, a group of Shi'as from the Ismaili branch entered the scene with ambitions to replace what they considered the illegitimate rule of the Abbasids.[19] By the early 10th century, these zealous missionaries, who called themselves **Fatimids** after Mohammed's daughter and the wife of Ali, the fourth *caliph*, spread their religion to Yemen and large sections of Egypt.

By 966, the Fatimids had successfully occupied Palestine and three years later conquered Egypt where they founded a new capital that they called Cairo. After the Fatimids opened the al-Azhar university in 970,[20] Egypt became the religious and intellectual center of the Muslim world. Despite their successes, the Fatimids faced much opposition from the Sunni Muslims and other Shi'a sects, especially when some of the Fatimid *caliphs* declared themselves the earthly incarnations of God.

Most destructive to the Fatimids' image, though, was the rule of the *caliph* **al-Hakim**, a murderous despot who made it a crime to sleep at night and work during the day, banned the making of women's shoes, ordered all dogs killed, forbad women from weeping at funerals and ordered Christians and Jews to wear crosses and bells, among other capricious demands. His persecution of Christian officials and especially the destruction of the Church of the Holy Sepulchre became the pretexts for the first Christian Crusade decades later. One evening, **al-Hakim** mysteriously disappeared (the **Druze**, who still worship the Fatimid *caliph*, say he was spirited to heaven) and the Fatimid Empire continued to rule for another 150 years until they were invaded by the **Seljuk Turks**, a band of Sunni warriors from Turkestan in Central Asia.

The Sunni Muslim descendants of a tribal chief named **Seljuk** (and predecessors of the Ottoman Turks) had been employed as mercenaries by the Abbasids before they became a military force in their own right. Under the leadership of Seljuk's grandson, **Tughril Beg**, who proclaimed himself Sultan in 1055, and his successor **Alp Arlam**, the Seljuks conquered Georgia, Armenia and much of Asia Minor. In 1070, they seized Syria and the holy cities of Palestine from the Fatimids and defeated the Byzantine Empire at **Manzikert**, a few miles from the Empire's capital (present-day Istanbul) the next year.

The invasion (along with concerns about the treatment of Christian pilgrims in Jerusalem) triggered the first Christian Crusade in 1095.

---

[19] Shi'as believed only blood relatives of the Prophet, especially those descended or related to the Prophet's cousin, Ali, were rightful rulers of the Muslim world.

[20] Al-Azhar is the oldest university in the world.

CRUSADES

By the end of the 10th century, the Muslim world was split into three realms with the respective rulers of each claiming to be the *caliph*. In the west, an Umayyad prince had survived the destruction of his family's empire and had set up his own Umayyad Empire centered in Cordoba, Spain (al-Andalus or Andalusia). In the east, the truncated Abbasid Dynasty ruled from Baghdad, and the Fatimids had established their own center of power in Cairo and ruled over Syria and Palestine.

A century later, the **Seljuks** seized Palestine and Syria from the Fatimids and were threatening the Byzantine Empire from Anatolia (present-day Turkey).

In Europe, meanwhile, the population was restive and the heads of the Christian church, which was split into the Eastern Orthodox (based in Constantinople, the Byzantine capital) and the western Roman Catholic Church, were competing over claims to authority over the Christian community.

All these worlds were about to collide at the beginning of the 11th century when the Byzantine king asked **Pope Urban II** of the western Catholic Church for help repelling the Muslim Seljuk Turks who were amassing on their border.

Hoping to assert the power of the Catholic Church in the Near East, redirect local hostilities towards an external enemy (the Muslims or *Saracens*) and riding on the wave of growing religious fervor, Pope Urban II decided to call on his subjects to reclaim the Holy Land from the "Muslim infidels." In 1095 the first of these Crusaders (or *Franks* as the Arabs called them) set out on a march to Jerusalem killing thousands of Jews (the Crusaders called them the "infidels at home" as opposed to the "infidels" in the East) along the way.

When these European zealots entered Jerusalem four years later, they set upon the city's inhabitants, slaughtering nearly all of the city's Jewish and Muslim inhabitants. The Church of the Holy Sepulchre (which had been destroyed by the Fatimid *caliph* **Malik** in 1009) was rebuilt beyond its original splendor and camps of crusaders were set up around Jerusalem. Even the Noble Sanctuary (site of the Temple of Solomon) was occupied by a group of monastic knights who called themselves the **Templars** (from the word "Temple") whose duty it was to protect Christian pilgrims and serve as the military arm of the crusaders. For nearly a century, western culture and the French language had replaced Islamic culture and the Arabic language, and military settlements and Christian churches replaced mosques and temples.

Sixty years after the First Crusaders entered Syria, a Seljuk prince, **Nureddin** (or **Nur al-Din**), captured Damascus and established a unified Muslim alliance in order to liberate the Middle East from the Christians. In Egypt meanwhile, the last Fatimid *caliph* had died in 1711 and was replaced by a Sunni Kurd, **Saladin** (**Salah al Din al Ayyubi**) who had once been employed by the Syrian prince Nureddin.

Unlike his Shi'ite predecessors, Saladin, was more interested in defending the Islamic culture from dissident Muslim sects and Christian European invaders, than just protecting the territory. He wanted Cairo to be the center of an

orthodox revival and built a number of prestigious *madrasas* (Muslim colleges) to advance the religion.

When Nureddin died in 1174, Saladin expanded his power base to Syria and thirteen years later, recaptured Jerusalem from the Christian crusaders at the Battle of the **Horns of Hittin**.

In strict observance of his Muslim faith, which encouraged humane and just treatment of prisoners of war, after his army defeated the Europeans Saladin treated the citizens of Jerusalem with respect and dignity and allowed them to leave the city peacefully. Eyewitnesses wrote that Saladin's squires offered to let elderly refugees ride on their horses as they departed and even carried children in their arms during the journey.

Saladin is still considered one of Islam's greatest heroes because of his courage, humility and piety and has been portrayed in a number of European novels as the model chivalrous knight. But his Ayyubid Dynasty and Muslim control over Palestine didn't last long after his death in 1193.

By 1203, a fourth Crusade had begun, which resulted in the capture of the Christian city of Constantinople by the Crusaders.

The **Mamelukes** took control over the Ayyubid dynasty in 1250.

MAMELUKES and MONGOLS

Saladin and his **Ayyubid** successors imported Turkic slaves to Egypt from the Black Sea region to serve as mercenary soldiers. After they were trained as cavalry soldiers and had converted to Islam, these slaves or *Mamelukes* (which translates as "owned") were given considerable freedom under their Ayyubid overlords and were even permitted to advance to positions of power and influence.

By 1250, the Mamelukes had become powerful enough to overthrow their masters like the Seljuk Turks had done centuries earlier. After the death of the last Ayyubid Sultan in 1249 and the assassination of his heir, a Mameluke general married the Sultan's widow ushering in three hundred years of Mameluke rule.

In the meantime in the eastern side of the Muslim Empire, another upheaval was taking place. A confederation of nomadic Mongolian tribes united by **Ghengis Khan** swept through Turkestan, Iran, Afghanistan, the Caucasus and Russia marauding and pillaging before the Khan's death in 1227. Under Ghengis' grandson, **Hulaga Khan**, the horde of **Mongols** invaded Baghdad and, in 1258, brought an end to the once-glorious Abbasid Empire.

After killing the *caliph* and hundreds of thousands of his subjects, the barbarian warriors devastated the land and destroyed the Abbasid's vast irrigation system. They also smashed many of the Empire's magnificent public works including libraries filled with priceless collections of cultural, scientific and technological records. Baghdad, like other cities that fell in the path of the destructive Mongol maelstrom, never completely recovered from the invasion.

In 1260, Hulagu's Mongol armies headed towards Syria leaving a trail of fires and destruction behind them. Once they arrived in Palestine, though, they were crushed by the Mamelukes near Nazareth and forced to retreat back to Asia before they could cause any further damage.

With the rival Abbasid Empire in ruins, the Mongols driven back and the last of the Crusaders routed from Palestine, the Mamelukes were free to rule the Middle East unopposed until the rise of the Ottomans in the 16th century.

OTTOMAN EMPIRE

In the wake of the Mongol's sweep from Asia to Palestine, another Muslim Dynasty emerged that would rule the territories surrounding the eastern half of the Mediterranean Sea until the 20th century.

The empire began as a small confederation of Turkish tribes who had migrated to Anatolia (present-day Turkey) to escape the Mongol invasion. Gathered in northwest Anatolia around a minor chieftain called **Osman**, these Muslim warriors (*ghazis*) were dedicated to the fight to capture land for Islam and were eager to expand their territory into the Roman Byzantine Empire across the border. In 1326, the **Osmanli** (or **Ottomans**) enjoyed their first victory by capturing the Byzantine town of Bursa.

To increase their military strength, the Ottoman *ghazis* hired and trained an elite corps of Christian soldiers called *Janissaries* (meaning "new troops" in Turkish) from Albania, Bosnia, Bulgaria and Armenia and launched new attacks along their European frontier.

By the end of the 14th century, the Ottomans had conquered Bulgaria, Macedonia and Serbia and were well on their way to capturing the Byzantine capital of Constantinople

When Constantinople finally fell to the invaders in 1453 the Ottomans renamed it **Istanbul** and rebuilt the devastated city into a fabulously wealthy Muslim center. The city's capture not only brought an end to the Roman Byzantine Empire, but made the Ottomans the new masters of the lucrative east-west trade routes.

Up to this point, the Ottomans' military focus had been directed against Christian Europe (in accordance with the *ghazis* policy of waging war against non-Muslims) but that was about to change.

Under the rule of **Selim the Grim** (1512-20) the Ottomans adopted the role of Islam's defenders, first from the influence of the heretical Shi'ite Muslims within the empire and in the Persian Safavid Empire, and then by "protecting" the territories under the Mamelukes from foreign invasion.

Although the Mamelukes were Sunni Muslims like the Ottomans, Selim believed that the Mameluke Dynasty was too weak and ill-equipped to defend the Muslim community from enemy attacks. As the only Islamic power strong enough to defend Islam's holiest cities, therefore, it was up to the Ottomans to bring the Islamic territories into their fold.

Consequently, in 1516 Selim took the Syrian cities of Aleppo, Damascus and Jerusalem from the Mamelukes, killed the Mameluke Sultan and declared Egypt and Syria to be under Ottoman control. He then made his way down the Arabian Peninsula to Medina and Mecca (which were also under Mameluke control) where he was given the keys to the cities by the **Sherif of Mecca** (the Keeper of Islam's holiest sites). After taking control of the holy cities, Selim added the designation of *caliph* to his title as Sultan, thereby assuming spiritual as well as secular leadership over the entire Muslim world.

Palestine in a Nutshell

Selim I had won control over some of the world's wealthiest trade routes and earned unprecedented spiritual authority. It was his son, **Suleiman**, though, who brought the Empire unparalleled prestige.

Under the rule of **Suleiman the Law-Giver** (called **Suleiman the Magnificent** by Europeans), the Ottoman Empire reached its zenith not only in terms of territorial growth (the size of the Empire more than doubled under Suleiman), but in cultural and intellectual achievements.

Suleiman, the brilliant military strategist, developed the best fleet in the Mediterranean and extended his rule west across North Africa, east along the upper Arabian Peninsula, north to Vienna and Russia's Crimea Coast, and south as far as Sudan.

As the head of the Muslim community, the Sultan paid special attention to the holy sites and ordered extensive restorations done at the **Dome of the Rock** (from where Mohammed had ascended to heaven). In Istanbul he built magnificent mosques, public baths, fountains, gardens and religious schools. In Jerusalem he rebuilt walls and gates that had been in ruins for centuries, reactivated the city's ancient aqueducts and made far-reaching improvements in other parts of the empire.

Until his death in 1566, Suleiman the Law-Giver presided over the most powerful nation in the world and left a legacy that touches the Arab world to this day. Although the Ottoman Empire continued to govern much of the Arab world until the 20th century, it never again saw such glory.

Ottoman Administration

The duty of the Sultan in the Ottoman Empire was to guarantee his people justice, to defend them from corrupt officials and unfair taxation (all laws and tax regulations were posted publicly to prevent fraud on the local level) and to protect their freedom to worship. The Sultan was also expected to uphold the Muslim Sacred Law (*Shari'a*) and was given absolute authority to govern according to the will of God.

In order to administer such a vast territory, the empire was divided into 30-40 *vilayets* or provinces each headed by a governor-general (or *wali*) who was directly responsible to the central government in Istanbul. The *vilayets* were themselves subdivided into *sanjaks*. Present-day Iraq, for instance, was once divided into four *vilayets* (Basra, Baghdad, Mosul and Shahrizure). Aleppo and Damascus were *vilayets* of Syria. And Palestine was comprised of the *vilayets* of Nablus, Akka and Jerusalem (which was governed directly by Constantinople because of its important religious and political status).

Although all the ethnically diverse territories in the empire ultimately fell under the authority of the central government through a bureaucratic chain of command, the Sultans were not anxious to impose Turkish culture on the distant populations. While Muslims were obliged to submit to *Sharia* Islamic law with regards to religious matters such as marriage, divorce, inheritance etc. non-Muslim citizens, organized into *millets* or religious minority communities, were permitted to follow their own religious laws.

In time, though, the freedoms exercised by people in these religious *millets*

(along with foreign intervention) began to provide them with economic advantages over their Muslim counterparts.

Decline

The gradual 300-year decline of the empire began in 1566 with the death of Suleiman. His heirs, who were often mired in successional disputes that frequently involved imprisoning or killing rival family members, were less capable administrators who were usually detached from the populace and unaware of international developments.

While the West experienced a cultural renaissance, the Ottomans stagnated intellectually. Muslim scholars were so convinced of the superiority of the Muslim and Ottoman civilization that they were closed to new ideas coming from the infidel West.

This isolation also prevented the introduction of western technological and scientific developments. Ancient agricultural methods and feudalism left the Ottomans unable to compete with the West in agricultural production and the infiltration of western manufactured goods made local craftsmen obsolete. The unfavorable trade balance caused the empire to deplete its stockpiles of gold -- which had already been losing its value worldwide due to the flood of cheap silver introduced by the Spanish from the New World (America).

In order to make up for the lost income and the devalued currency, new and heavier taxes were imposed on the people – with the tax burden falling most heavily on the peasants. By this time, the process of tax collecting had become corrupt. Most of the tax-collecting posts had been bought by officials who, in turn, squeezed extra taxes from the populace for their own gain.

The Ottoman Empire's economy was also adversely affected when the West began using new trade-routes to India and Asia that bypassed the Ottoman Empire.

In order to lure European commerce back to the Empire, the Ottomans offered special trade agreements (called **Capitulations**) to foreign merchants that gave them certain financial and judicial privileges that were not granted to the local population. Traders were given the same amount of autonomy as members of the religious *millets* which had fallen increasingly under the control of European countries.

As Ottoman authority weakened, the European states extended their influence in the Empire by claiming to represent the interests of the religious minority groups. France claimed to be the protectors of all Catholics living in the Empire, Russia claimed rights of protection over the Orthodox communities and the British claimed to be the protectors of the Jews, Druze (a Muslim sect comprised of followers of Fatimid *caliph* al-Hakim) and Protestants.

The trade advantages and protectionist claims gradually transformed into foreign exploitation. Foreign loans granted to the Ottoman Empire were accompanied by stipulations and the European nations gained leverage by claiming activities within the country were intended to protect their religious protectorates. In time, European countries owned and ran banks, railways, mining companies and other businesses in the Ottoman Empire which was falling

deeply into debt.

Along with diminished cultural prestige and economic decline, the Ottoman Empire lost its military strength when its *Janissaries*, once the world's most effective military unit, became too powerful and turned on their masters. Once composed of young celibate Christian captives, the members of the elite *Janissary* corps became more and more autonomous until they became a state within a state that was strong enough to stage palace coups and influence governmental policy. The military force was finally disbanded by the Sultan **Mahmud II** and all the soldiers were killed or banished. The troops were replaced by local amateur recruits.

Without a reliable military force, the Ottomans were vulnerable to attacks by European armies and the empire slowly began to lose territory from the 17th century until its final disintegration after World War I.

Catherine the Great, Empress of Russia, who dreamed of creating a neo-Byzantine Empire with its capital at Constantinople, tried to break up the Ottoman Empire through a series of Russo-Turkish wars (from 1768-1792) that won Russia sovereignty over the Crimea and cemented Russia's hold on the northern coast of the Black Sea.

A few years later, **Napoleon** entered Egypt and Palestine in an attempt to block Britain's passage to India but the French forces were defeated by the British before they could take full control of the Ottoman territories. Their brief occupation introduced a number of western ideas to the Middle East (for example, French Revolutionary ideals of egalitarianism, liberty and brotherhood spread at this time) and exposed the Turkish Empire's military and technological inferiority to the West. It also marked the beginning of the struggle between Britain and France to control the region and keep it out of the hands of the Russians.

Crimean War

In 1854, Western interference in Ottoman affairs turned into a war between the European powers who had been quarreling over who should have authority over the holy places in Jerusalem. **Tsar Nicholas I** claimed that Russia, as protector of the Empire's Orthodox Christians, had the right to protect the Christian shrines in Jerusalem and Nazareth while the French, as protectors of the Catholics, believed it was their right.

To back up their claims, the Tsar's Russian troops moved into present-day Romania and other parts of the Ottoman Empire triggering British involvement. The British harbored a constant fear that if the Russians defeated the Ottomans, Russia would dominate the valuable sea routes to Central Asia and block British passage to its valuable colony of India. From 1854 to1856, France joined Britain in a war against the Russians that was fought around the Crimean peninsula.[21]

Egypt

The French occupation of Egypt in the late 18th century destroyed the authority of the Mameluke *beys* (leaders) who had become tyrants under the nominal

---

21 The **Treaty of Paris**, signed in 1856, ended the war and made the Black Sea a neutral region. The appalling treatment of wounded soldiers during the Crimean War inspired Florence Nightingale to push for reforms in the British military health-care system.

control of Ottoman Turks. In their place, the Egyptian people asked military leader **Mohammed Ali** to take control in order to push back the British who were trying to restore the Mamelukes to power. In 1805 Mohammed Ali was recognized by the Ottoman Sultan as the Viceroy (or Pasha) of Egypt and he set out to modernize his new realm. During his reign, Ali turned Egypt into a major Mediterranean power by overseeing the construction of new irrigation works, factories and technical schools, modernizing agricultural methods, vaccinating the population against smallpox and other epidemics, improving the military and conducting other advancements.

In 1831, the Egyptian leader sent his son, **Ibrahim Pasha** to conquer Syria which he forcefully accomplished. By 1833, Ibrahim had become the governor in Syria and tried to introduce a number of reforms as his father had done in Egypt. But the imposition of central authority (which challenged the rule of the local notables and rural shaykhs), forced conscription and the heavy taxation imposed to pay for the reforms were met with rebellion. By 1840, with the help of the subjugated people, the Ottomans came and re-imposed control over Syria and Palestine.

Twenty years later, the Egyptians signed an agreement with the French Vice-Consul to Egypt, **Ferdinand de Lesseps**, to build and operate a canal through **Suez** Isthmus linking the Mediterranean Sea and the Red Sea. A company was formed by French shareholders using French capital and employing French managers to supervise the construction of the canal and Egypt was expected to provide unpaid laborers and land grants in exchange for its share of the holdings. The Canal Company was given a concession over the canal for ninety-nine years from the time the canal was built in 1869. Eight years later, the Egyptian Viceroy faced bankruptcy and sold the Egyptian shares to Britain for four million pounds.

Foreign ownership over the canal, which became an invaluable waterway from Europe to the East, along with Egypt's indebtedness to France and Britain, gave the European countries a direct interest in Egyptian affairs and an excuse to take financial control of the territory in 1883. From their foothold in Egypt, both Britain and France maintained a powerful presence in the Middle East.

The "Sick Man of Europe"
By the end of the 19th century, the Ottoman Empire was considered the "sick man of Europe." All its North African and European territories to the Aegean Sea had been lost and the rest of the Empire was artificially kept intact through the intervention of the West.[22] Its disintegration was inevitable and Britain, France, Russia and other countries were waiting like vultures to claim their shares of the Empire once it collapsed.

Even the subjects of the Ottoman Empire, overburdened by crippling taxes, suffering under the rule of corrupt local rulers and resentful of the central government's sudden effort to impose Turkish culture[23] on its mostly Arab popu-

---

[22] Britain believed that the Ottoman Empire needed to be preserved and supported so that it would not fall into Russian hands.

[23] In an effort to modernize the empire in the mid-19th century, the imperial rulers decided to try to "Turkify" the population, for example by imposing Turkish as the language of education.

lation, were ready to see the rest of the Empire carved up into independent states. The Arabs, like the Greeks, Serbs, Armenians, Croats, Albanians and many other nationalist groups before them, wanted the right to decide their own political status or form of government.

Palestine in the Ottoman Period

From the time *caliph* **Umar** entered Jerusalem in 638 Palestine had continuously been in Islamic hands and through most of that time, Jews and Christians ("people of the book" or *dhimmies*) were granted the freedom to worship and to observe their own religious laws. When the Ottomans took over in 1516, they continued that policy of religious tolerance.

Christians and Jews were required to pay a special tax (*jizya*) that was not paid by Muslims and in return they were exempt from military duty. Each religious community (*millet*) also maintained its own places of worship, schools, courts, welfare system and, in some cases, built their own roads. The *millets* were happy to have control over these institutions and the Ottoman authorities were happy to be relieved of the responsibility. As the empire weakened, though, these liberties were exploited by foreign countries who used access to the religious communities to get a foothold in the Levant (the eastern Mediterranean area).

In 1774, according to the **Treaty of Kuchuk Kainarji** that ended the Turko-Russian wars, Russia was given the right to represent the Greek Orthodox subjects of the Sultan. The treaty became the basis of later Russian claims of protection rights over all the Christians in the Ottoman Empire. Not to be outdone by their Russian foes, the French eventually demanded the right to "protect" the Empire's Roman Catholics and the British became protectors of the Jews, Druze and Protestants. As rights were extended to the religious communities the hold of their foreign guardians deepened. Each country had its own reasons for wanting to maintain a heavy presence in the Middle East.

In the late 18th century, **Napoleon Bonaparte** hoped to hurt Britain financially and militarily by occupying territories along their route to India. Napoleon first crushed the Mamelukes (who still had power in Egypt under Ottoman tutelage) and then moved into Palestine (a point of pride for Napoleon who felt he was following in the footsteps of Alexander the Great).

Napoleon was stopped by the Ottomans with British help at Acre (or Akko in Arabic and Hebrew) but his influence was felt long after his troops returned home. Napoleon was so sure that he would be victorious in the Holy Land that he brought a thousand civilians along with him to modernize the territory for future European settlement. Artists, botanists, zoologists, economists, surveyors and other professionals brought back a detailed 22-volume compendium of information about Palestine and Egypt which helped arouse romantic interest in the Orient and sparked new desire to visit the area.

Napoleon's presence in the Empire also gave the Ottomans a first-hand view of modern military techniques and weaponry and exposed the Middle East to French Revolutionary ideals of religious equality, nationalism and liberty. The

experience deeply affected the Ottoman leadership as well as the religious minority groups (Bonaparte's promise to make Palestine a Jewish homeland under French protection was a forerunner to future European Jewish patronage).

Before the French invasion, the Ottomans were resistant to change believing that their Muslim institutions (which were based on divine tenets) were far superior to those of the non-Muslim West. After Napoleon's occupation, though, the Ottomans realized how backward they had become and began to reform the empire's fundamental institutions in Western fashion with the help of imported foreign experts. The *Janissaries*, for example, were replaced with a new army, religious and secular institutions were reorganized to reflect Western-style administration, schools and academies were opened that taught modern European subjects and even dress styles were modernized.

Even more aggressive changes were made in Egypt after the Mamelukes had been defeated by the French. **Mohammed Ali**, an officer of the Ottoman forces, stepped into the power vacuum as Egypt's new Pasha (military/civil leader) in 1805 and ambitiously set about modernizing the region. Although nominally subordinate to the Ottoman leadership, he defied Turkish authority in 1831 by sending an army led by his son, **Ibrahim Pasha**, to occupy Palestine.

In the nine years of occupation (1831-40) the Egyptians established law and order (for years the area had been plagued by bloody inter-tribal wars), centralized control, drained marshes, secularized the judicial system, opened a number of schools and organized building projects. But the reforms angered the local ruling classes and religious leaders, whose authority had been challenged by the new overlords.

The local residents also objected to the introduction of military conscription, the imposition of heavy taxes (collected to pay for reforms) and economic competition that accompanied the immigration of thousands of Egyptian immigrants. The increasing burdens provoked peasant rebellions which were brutally quelled by the Egyptian government and impelled the Ottomans to try to win back the territory.

With help from the British navy and other foreign troops (whose interests were also threatened by the Egyptian occupation), the Ottomans ejected the Egyptians and regained control over Palestine and Syria. In return for Britain's help, though, the Ottomans were obliged to augment the rights of foreigners in the Empire.

The consequent **Imperial Rescript of Gulhane** (*Hatt-i-Sherif*) issued in 1839 guaranteed security of life, honor and property for all subjects in the Empire, established a fixed and fair tax system and reduced military service to five years. Most importantly, the reforms (or *Tanzimat*) raised the status of Jews and Christians (formerly considered second-class citizens) by making them equal citizens under the law.

The new rights attracted Jewish and Christian immigrants and allowed

Palestine in a Nutshell

European nations to further penetrate the Ottoman Empire by claiming their presence was necessary to protect the interests of the religious minorities. Consulates, schools, hostels, hospitals, charitable institutions and religious centers sprang up in Jerusalem and the Palestinian seaports to serve the growing number of pilgrims, missionaries and Jewish settlers (who began trickling into Palestine in the mid-19th century). The foreign nationals had so thoroughly established themselves in the holy cities of Palestine, in fact, that they began to compete over religious jurisdictions. It was just this type of rivalry between the Russians and French over control of Christian religious sites in Jerusalem that sparked the **Crimean War** in 1854.

From Jerusalem, the Crimean War escalated into a Russia invasion of the Ottoman Empire's northern territories. The *Sublime Porte* (the Ottoman court) was again forced to call on the British and French to help defend the Empire and again extended rights to minorities as a result. In 1856 non-Muslims were granted the same privileges as Muslims in terms of military service, taxation, judicial law, property rights and education thereby ending centuries of Muslim hegemony over non-believers living within Islamic borders.

The Crimean War also plunged the Ottomans deeper into debt prompting the government to reform the empire's land laws. By reforming land ownership laws and reasserting the state's legal rights to property, the Ottomans hoped to generate a steady stream of property tax income and earn profits from the sale of state land.

The reform divided land into four categories: church land or *waqf* (including land owned and managed by foreign religious minorities), private land, unoccupied land and state land. Fields that remained fallow for three years became the property of the state (which meant that the state had the right to confiscate acres of land that had been occupied by Bedouin nomads) and could be sold to the highest bidder when the Empire's coffers were low.

State land that was put on the market was sold at public auctions that were eagerly attended by foreigners -- especially Jews who bought large tracts of land with money donated by Zionist organizations in order to accommodate Jewish immigrants.

The new reforms formally set land taxes at 10% but corrupt officials frequently collected much more than that as they had before the land laws were established. Landowners burdened with crippling taxes (sometimes up to 40%) and small harvests were often forced to borrow money at high interest rates to purchase seeds for the following year's crops. The combined burdens of taxation and interest loans plunged many farmers so deeply into debt that they were forced to give up their land to their creditors. The new owners would then hire the former landowners to cultivate their fields as tenant-farmers.

By the end of the 19th century, most Palestinian land was in the hands of minority religious groups or was owned by the state or large absentee landowners who readily sold the land to wealthy buyers – especially the Zionist Jews.

WORLD WAR I

By the end of the 19th century, Britain and France had established a strong foothold in the Levant through their patronage of minority religious groups and their Ottoman host had become the "sick man of Europe" to the rest of the world. A quarter of the Empire's territories had seceded and the Turkish rulers were too weak and indebted to defend themselves against invaders without outside help. The Empire's survival, in fact, depended on the very people who had positioned themselves take over once it fell apart.

The material and administrative inferiority of the once-glorious Turkish state in relation to the Christian West was particularly humiliating to Muslims who blamed the outdated Sultanate and foreign pressure for the decline.

Despite attempts by **Sultan Abd-ul-Hamid II** and his predecessors to reform and modernize the empire, the autocratic Sultan couldn't compete with the liberal and nationalistic ideas that had inspired the breakaway republics to fight for their independence (the Greeks, Macedonians, Balkans etc.) and provoked young Turkish officers and students to rebel against the old order within the empire.

In 1908, a group of students and officers, organized as the "**Young Turks**" and ruled by the **Committee of Union and Progress** (CUP), rebelled against the archaic Ottoman ruling class and became the de facto rulers of the empire. The members of the chauvinistic CUP immediately initiated a program of Turkification (promoting Turkish history, culture and language) in the mostly Arab states, which further alienated a population that was already suffering from economic crises, corrupt local governments and foreign competition.

One of the most tragic acts committed by the leaders of the short-lived "Young Turk" movement was their effort to consolidate and expand Turkish rule by brutally exterminating the Armenian population living in the Turanian lands in the east. Under the Ottomans, the Armenians had become a prosperous minority which challenged the Young Turks' ambition of being the wealthiest and most powerful ethnic group in the empire. The Armenians (who were sympathetic to rival Russia) also straddled a strategic territory in the east that the CUP had planned to annex. To rid the country of their competitors the Turks systematically deported and massacred the entire Armenian community from 1915 to 1921 and expropriated the property they left behind. This annihilation (which the Turks deny took place) is still commemorated by Armenians worldwide on April 24th as Martyr's Day.

At the onset of the First World War, the Turks also decided to shift allegiances from the Empire's traditional allies, Britain and France, to the Germans - in part to counter the Russian forces. By joining the Central Powers (Germany, Italy and Austria-Hungary) against the Allies (Britain, France and Russia), the Turks gave the British the excuse they needed to finally overtake the Ottoman Empire.

In order to bring the Empire to a swift end, the British urged the already disaf-

fected Arabs to stage a revolt against their Turkish rulers with the implication that they would be granted independence once the Empire had collapsed.

In October, 1915, the British High Commissioner, **Sir Henry McMahon** assured **Sherif Hussein ibn Ali,**[24] patriarch of the Hashemite family and Ottoman governor of Islam's holiest cities, Mecca and Medina (in present-day Saudi Arabia), that the British government was prepared to recognize and support the establishment of an independent Arab state under Hashemite rule in the Arab provinces of the Ottoman Empire in return for Arab support.

To help coordinate the rebellion, the British army sent **T.E. Lawrence** (better known as **Lawrence of Arabia**), an intelligence officer who had become an expert on Arab affair. With Sherif Hussein's son, **Faisal**, Lawrence led an Arab army across Arabia to battle the Turkish troops while the British fought them on the western front. After the Turks had been driven out of Jerusalem in the **Battle of al-Aqaba** in 1917, the ragtag Arab army joined the allied forces of **General Allenby** and flanked the British forces as they moved north to Damascus. In 1918, two days after the siege of Damascus and the installment of **Faisal ibn Ali** as Syria's king, Lawrence and the Arabs learned that the British had made a conflicting agreement with the French two years earlier regarding the Ottoman territories.

The **Sykes-Picot** agreement, which had been signed secretly by the French and British governments in 1916, laid out plans to carve up the Ottoman territories into French and British spheres of influence. According to the agreement, the European powers were "prepared to recognize and protect an independent Arab state or a confederation of Arab states" but retained quasi-colonial authority over pre-determined areas. France would exercise direct control over an area roughly corresponding to present-day Lebanon and the southwest portion of Turkey and have an "influence" over Syria and northern Iraq. Britain would have direct control over the southern portion of present-day Iraq (including Baghdad) and have "influence" over Jordan and North Arabia. Palestine was to become an International zone.

At the **Versailles Peace Conference** (also called the "Paris Peace Conference") ending World War I in 1919 (which T.E. Lawrence had attended on behalf of the Arabs) the secret agreement between Britain and France was revealed and criticized by American president **Woodrow Wilson**. The colonial tone of the Sykes-Picot agreement went against the notion of worldwide national self-determination which had been promoted in Wilson's "**Fourteen Points**" speech delivered in January 1918 and it betrayed the aim of the League of Nations. As a compromise, therefore, it was agreed that the Ottoman territories would become "mandates" of Britain and France while they were being prepared for future self rule; that is, the European countries would have the right to temporarily administer the government and affairs of the Ottoman territories until it was decided that they could function independently.

---

[24] As a descendant of Mohammed, Sherif Hussein was one of the only legitimate religious figures who could challenge the Ottoman *caliph* (who was still considered the defender of the faith).

To add to the confusion, Britain had also agreed to establish a homeland for the Jews in Palestine in return for their efforts in World War I. In a 1917 letter from British Foreign Secretary Lord Balfour to Lord Rothschild (see the "**Balfour Declaration**" in Israel section), the Jews were promised a "national home" in Palestine as long as the establishment of such a homeland would not "prejudice the civil and religious rights of existing non-Jewish communities in Palestine."

Both the terms of the Balfour Declaration and Sykes-Picot were reaffirmed in April 1920 at the **San Remo** conference which decided the final fate of the former Ottoman-ruled Arab lands of the Middle East. As a result, Britain received the mandate for Palestine (including the area that would be called "Transjordan") and present-day Iraq, while France would have authority over Syria and Lebanon -- thereby expelling the government of Sherif Hussein's son, **Faisal ibn Ali**, which had been set up in Damascus when the Arabs captured the city in 1918 (see "Syria" section).

In an effort to fulfill the promise made to Sherif Hussein by Sir Henry McMahon in 1917, the British installed the deposed and exiled King Faisal as the ruler of Iraq and made his brother, **Abdullah**, the Emir of Transjordan.

By dividing the Ottoman Empire into small, unstable states headed by foreign rulers who depended on the West for legitimacy (both Faisal and Abdullah were Saudis), the occupiers had successfully ensured that the Middle East would no longer pose a viable threat to the West. The European powers, moreover, were now in a position to exercise great economic, political and military control over the Middle East.

The deceptions and occupation of the former Ottoman Empire left a lasting sense of bitterness within the Arab community and fueled the determination of nationalists to reunite the Arab world into a powerful state that could again counter the West. This ideology became the basis for modern pan-Arab movements led by the Ba'ath Party of Syria and Iraq, Gamal Abdul Nasser of Egypt and others.

MANDATE

To secure its victory over the Central Powers in World War I, Britain entered into three contradictory agreements regarding the territories of the Ottoman Empire:

In the **Sykes-Picot** settlement of 1916, the French and British agreed to divide the territories between them with France exercising control over Syria and Lebanon and Britain dominating Transjordan (Jordan) and Iraq.

In the 1915 **McMahon-Hussein** agreement the British also promised that the Arab portions of the Ottoman Empire would become independent under the rule of the Saudi Arab Hashemite family in return for launching an Arab revolt against the Ottoman Turks.

In yet another treaty, the **Balfour Declaration** written in 1917, the British promised the Jews that they would be granted a national homeland in Palestine if they aided the British in World War I.

From the moment Palestine came under British control in December 1917, therefore, the question of entitlement was an issue.

Zionism

Although Jews had been living and settling in Palestine throughout the Ottoman period, Jewish claims of absolute entitlement to the land didn't emerge until the advent of the modern Zionist movement in the late 19th century (see "Zionism" in Israel section). The Zionists renewed claims that as descendants of Abraham's son Isaac, God had promised the Jews (the "chosen people") the land of Canaan ("Zion" or "Eretz-Israel"). From the time the Jews were first exiled from Judah (in present-day West Bank) to Babylon in the seventh century B.C. the dream that the Israelites would one day return to their "homeland" -- especially to their ancient capital of Jerusalem where the Holy Temple (the site of the Noble Sanctuary) had once held the Ark of the Covenant -- was kept alive through their daily prayers and rituals.

After centuries of living in the Diaspora (the scattering or "dispersion" of Jews from Palestine after the second century), Jews had made homes in all corners of the world and had successfully integrated into many of the most progressive cities in Western Europe -- in some cases, enjoying great wealth and power in their adopted countries (most notably the Rothschilds in Britain). Jews living in Eastern Europe, on the other hand, were suffering the effects of growing anti-Semitism and a series of *pogroms* (organized persecutions) in Russia.

The desire of the Jews in the West to help their Eastern European brothers was compounded by the recognition that the Jews, no matter how assimilated politically, socially and financially, were inherently seen as dangerous outsider s in all places of exile -- a fact that was made all the more evident during the famous **Dreyfus Affair** in France. In 1884, a Jewish officer named Alfred Dreyfus was accused of a crime that he had not committed. Although he was eventually acquitted once the true culprits were discovered, the case exposed underlying anti-Semitic sentiments in a nation that had been built on the ideals of equali-

ty, fraternity and liberty.

Out of the ashes of the Dreyfus trial and in the midst of waves of anti-Semitic pogroms emerged an intellectual movement called **Zionism** that advocated the return of Jews to their homeland of *Eretz Israel* with borders that included Palestine, the western part of Jordan, southern Lebanon and southern Syria. Foremost among these intellectual theorists was **Theodore Herzl** who outlined a plan for the creation of a Jewish commonwealth in his book *Judenstaat* ("Jewish State").

With the help of Jewish philanthropists (Baron de Rothschild and Sir Moses Montefiore among them) a number of Jews set out to realize the Zionist dream by repatriating the "people without a land" (Jews) in what they claimed was a "land without people" (Palestine).

However, the designated "people-less" land was in fact a relatively well-populated area with a thriving agrarian-based society. In order to establish the idyllic farm communities envisioned in the Zionist proposals (precursors to *Kibbutzim*), land had to be purchased from its landowners and from the state (acres of land were sold to Jews through auctions hosted by the financially ailing Ottoman Empire).

Jews under the Mandate

When the British took control over Palestine after World War I, they had incorporated the tenets of the **Balfour Declaration** into the terms of the mandate thereby formally endorsing Jewish settlement of the land. British decrees allowing free exercise of all forms of worship and introducing Hebrew as a state-recognized language further attracted hundreds of thousands of Jewish immigrants between 1922 and 1946 nearly tripling the Jewish population from 11% of Palestine's total inhabitants in the first year of the mandate to 31% two decades later.

Aided by huge sources of funds from wealthy Zionist organizations and supported by the British government, the Jewish immigrants were able to develop institutions to facilitate settlement and govern the new arrivals. Jewish workers were represented by labor unions (in 1920, the **Histadrut**, the General Federation of Jewish Labor, was created to provide health benefits, pensions and social services to Jewish workers) and were hired *en masse* by new Jewish business owners. Hebrew schools were opened with modern curricula taught by teachers who had been educated in higher educational institutions abroad. And Zionist institutions like the **Hadassah Medical Organization** (HMO) established hospitals, clinics, pharmacies and other radical programs in cities with high concentrations of Jews.

Palestinians under the Mandate

In contrast, the indigenous Palestinians, who still vastly outnumbered the Jewish inhabitants, were losing their homes and jobs as land they had worked on for generations passed into the hands of the new immigrants. Initially, agricultural workers and peasants were retained as tenant farmers by the new land-

lords, but they were soon replaced by incoming Jewish workers.

Left landless and jobless, many of the displaced Palestinian farmers were forced to look for jobs in the cities where new Jewish-owned businesses offered opportunities for employment. As in the countryside, though, Jewish workers (who were often better educated[25] and hence commanded bigger salaries) were hired over Palestinians. Palestinian shantytowns which began to surface around some of the coastal cities, demonstrated the growing disparity between the well-funded Jews arriving from Europe and the indigenous Arab population.

Political Representation
The British also authorized the establishment of a Jewish Agency to act as the official representative of the Jewish people in dealings with the British administration and world powers. Its primary function was to negotiate on behalf of the Jewish settler community but it gradually acted like a state within a state with its own organized and well-financed political agencies, military and intelligence units and social and economic programs.

Although the Palestinian Arabs were encouraged by the British to establish a parallel organization, they refused since an equivalent agency would imply their acceptance that the Jewish settlers (who still only represented a small fraction of the Palestinian population) had equal rights to the land. A fair governing body, the Arabs contended, would be comprised of a representative body of delegates who would speak for the whole population. Such a government would offer the Palestinians a strong numerical advantage and thus was rejected by the Zionists.

As an alternative, Palestinians from Arab villages and towns convened in 1919 in the first unofficial **Palestine Congress** held in Jerusalem to discuss the question of Zionism and the political future of Palestine. Fearing that the Jews planned to create a wholly Jewish nation by displacing all its indigenous inhabitants, the attendees of the Congress sent a memorandum to the Paris Peace Conference (where the Allied nations were meeting to negotiate the terms ending World War I) opposing the Balfour Declaration and demanding independence as promised in the McMahon-Hussein agreement.

To investigate these demands, the U.S. sent a group of delegates (the King-Crane Commission) who determined that the "extreme Zionist program must be greatly modified" because a "national home for the Jewish people is not equivalent to making Palestine into a Jewish State and the erection of such a Jewish state would be accomplished with the gravest trespass upon civil and religious rights of existing non-Jewish communities in Palestine."

When the wishes of the Palestinians were ignored at the Peace Conference, despite the findings of the King-Crane Commission, the Palestinians discontent erupted into political demonstrations and riots.

---

25 In *Essays on the Structure of the Jewish Economy in Palestine and Israel* written in 1968, Robert Szereszewski estimated that 90% of Jews were literate during the British Mandate period compared to 30% of the Palestinians.

In another Palestinian Congress held in December, 1920, the Palestinian National Congress elected a 24-member Executive Committee that included members of the top two competing families in Jerusalem, the Husseinis and the Nashashibis. The Congress again rejected the Balfour Declaration, a program for a Jewish National Home and mass Jewish immigration and again sent a delegation to Britain to persuade the Colonial Office to change its pro-Zionist stance.

Instead of acceding to their demands, the British government issued the Churchill White Paper that reaffirmed the Balfour Declaration and stated that Palestine west of the Jordan was not among the areas promised to **Sherif Hussein** in 1915. It did, however, insist that a Jewish national home in Palestine would not be accomplished at the expense or exclusion of the Arab population, language or culture and limited Jewish immigration so that it would not "exceed economic capacity of the country at the time to absorb new arrivals."

In October, 1923, the British once again offered to create an Arab Agency comparable to the Jewish Agency but again the Palestinian leaders refused in favor of an elected representative legislative council that would serve the whole population. Without official status, the Palestinian Arab Executive was limited in its advisory capabilities and differences within the Committee (between the rival clans of the Husseinis and the Nashashibis) politically paralyzed the Palestinians even more.

The British had named **al-Hajj Amin al-Husseini** as *mufti*[26] and president of the **Supreme Muslim Council** (which administered the Islamic holy sites [*waqfs*], Sharia courts, mosques, schools etc.). The appointment of Husseini over the Nashashibi candidate provoked the Nashashibis to form competing organizations and encouraged the creation of independent peasant parties. Politically divided, the Palestinian community was too disorganized to challenge the cohesive Zionist institutions.

Wailing Wall Crisis

While the Palestinian leaders were ineffectually canvassing for better political terms, the impoverished peasants were suffering from high taxation rates, displacement by Jewish immigrants, inadequate educational opportunities and adverse living conditions. Adding to their distress, Palestine was hit with a drought in 1926, an earthquake in 1927 and a plague of locusts in 1928. By the end of the decade, moreover, a worldwide depression affected the economies of all countries.

The despair that had been simmering below the surface came to a head in 1929 after a crisis at the Wailing Wall (the only remaining portion of the Solomon Temple and holiest site to the Jews) in Jerusalem. A screen that had been erected at the site by Jews to divide male and female worshippers was seen by Muslims as an alteration of the holy site that was shared by both faiths (the Wailing Wall is also the Western Wall containing the Muslim's Noble Sanctuary

---

[26] A jurist who interprets Muslim law.

- see diagram in "Jerusalem" section). The disagreement erupted into violence which quickly spread to other parts of Palestine.

The British responded by sending two more Commissions, the Shaw Commission and Hope-Simpson Commission, to investigate the causes of the conflict. The Shaw report determined that the tension was the result of Western disregard for Arab political and national aspirations, Palestinian fear of economic domination by Jews who appeared to have unlimited funding from abroad and contradictory promises made by the British to both Jews and Arabs. Sir John Hope-Simpson found that there was not enough land to support continual immigration and a growing Palestinian Arab population and recommended that Jewish immigration be stopped.

The report also found that tenant farmers were falling deeper into debt due to taxation and loan interest payments; the increasing land sales to Jews were creating a class of landless Arab peasants and urban unemployment (since immigrant Jews were being hired over local Arabs) and declining wages were hurting Arabs in the cities.

The resultant **Passfield White Paper** considered the assessments noted in the Shaw and Hope-Simpson reports and criticized several Jewish institutions that promoted Jewish employment over Arab. It proposed that Jews would need to get permission from British authorities before purchasing land and it restricted Jewish immigration. The decisions were clearly pro-Arab and vigorously opposed by Zionists worldwide compelling British Prime Minister **Ramsay MacDonald** to repudiate and reverse the policy in a letter to one of the leading Zionists (called the "black letter" by Arabs). MacDonald's actions infuriated the Palestinians and heightened anti-British sentiments.

After another wave of Jewish immigrants arrived in Palestine following the rise of Nazism in Germany and crippling new land taxes and shrinking incomes worsened an already desperate economic situation, the Palestinians rose up again. This time, the demonstration involved all levels of Palestinian society from Bedouins (Arab nomads) to middle-class businessmen and professionals and was targeted against the British as well as the Jews.

To coordinate the 1936 strike, the Palestinian Executive Committee reorganized into the **Arab Higher Committee** representing all political factions under the leadership of Hajj Amin al-Husseini. Within a few months, the strike turned into armed insurrection by guerrilla bands whose only advantage over the well-armed British was their knowledge of the terrain and the use of guerrilla tactics. The British countered by imposing curfews and employing harsh emergency measures. After the insurrection, the British punished entire villages for their role in the uprising, disarmed the population and demanded compensation for damages caused by the unrest.

Once order had been restored, the British appointed a Royal Commission under **Lord Peel** to find a solution to the Palestinian grievances. He recommended restricting Jewish immigration to 12,000 people per year and, deter-

mining that the interest of the Jews and Arabs were irreconcilable, suggested that the British partition the territory into a Jewish state and an Arab state with British administration in Jerusalem.

The Palestinians were outraged by the proposition of dividing their land to accommodate a minority of Jewish immigrants and intensified the revolt.

This time, the British troops (who outnumbered the Palestinians ten to one) crushed the rebellion, imprisoned thousands of rebels, exiled the Palestinian leaders and outlawed all parties and political activity. In the end, the Palestinians were left demoralized and politically, militarily and economically powerless to resist the Jews and the colonial British.

Britain's last-ditch effort to maintain order in Palestine by issuing the **White Paper of 1939** which restricted Jewish immigration to 75,000 Jews over five years and offered to grant independence to Palestine within 10 years, invited the most bitter international criticism Britain had yet encountered. The cap on immigration had come at precisely the moment when Jews most needed a homeland -- during and after the Jewish Holocaust in Germany.

As the world was trying to persuade Britain to relax its restrictions, Jews within the country organized themselves into militant cells that tried to terrorize the British into leaving so that a Jewish commonwealth could be established in Palestine.

In 1941, the Jewish militia organization **Irgun** attempted to assassinate al-Hajj amin al-Husseini, leader of the Arab Higher Committee. In 1944, the terrorist Jewish group, **Stern Gang**, assassinated **Lord Moyne**, the British minister in Egypt. And in1946, Jewish terrorists blew up the **King David Hotel, the** headquarters of the British Mandate authorities in Jerusalem. With their numbers augmented by thousands of Jewish veterans of World War II, the Jewish community had become strong enough militarily to conduct a ferocious revolt against the British and the Palestinians.

By 1947, the British, burdened by anarchy in Palestine and condemnation abroad, finally decided to relinquish control over its Palestinian mandate and handed power over to the United Nations. Like Lord Peel, the UN leaders determined that the only solution to the turmoil in Palestine would be to partition the territory into an Arab and Jewish state. According to the terms of **UN Resolution 181**, the Jews (still only 31% of the population) would be awarded roughly 55% of the land while the Palestinian majority would receive only 45% of their homeland.

In May, 1948 (two months before their scheduled departure), the British pulled out of the Levant. In their haste, they left the Palestinians politically weakened (most of the Palestinian leadership had been killed or exiled), defenseless (the population had been disarmed) and impoverished. The Jews, on the other hand, had developed organized institutions that were prepared to assume governmental functions. They also had wealth and a well-armed, disciplined military at their disposal.

Palestine in a Nutshell

AL-NAKBAH (The Catastrophe) 1948

The United States and the Soviet Union recognized the state of Israel almost immediately after Zionist leader **David Ben-Gurion** declared its independence on May 14, 1948. But "Israel" was not recognized by the Palestinians or the Arab states.

United in their commitment to win independence for all Arabs under alien rule, the independent Arab nations of Egypt, Syria, Lebanon, Jordan, Iraq, Saudi Arabia and Yemen did what they could to prevent the Jewish minority in Palestine from creating a viable Jewish state. By boycotting all Jewish products and companies that did business with Israel, they hoped to cripple the country economically and after Ben-Gurion's declaration of independence, the Arab states came to the aid of the Palestinians by declaring war on the Zionists.

The combined Arab powers, though, were no match for the highly organized **Israeli Defense Force** (which had absorbed all the underground forces including the Jewish terrorist militias **Irgun** and **Stern Gang**). The Zionists were fully prepared to conduct a full-scale war with unified leadership, general conscription, modern weaponry and air power. The United Arab forces, on the other hand, had no comprehensive strategy, poor and defective weaponry and no overall leadership. Each country was fighting its own war against the Zionist enemies -- in some cases with territorial ambitions in mind.

By the time the U.N. sponsored cease-fire was declared in May, 1949, the Zionists had conquered territory beyond that which was allocated by the U.N. partition plan. The acquired land was incorporated into the new borders of the state of Israel.

Initially, the **Egyptians** refused to negotiate a peace agreement claiming this was not a war against a sovereign state but rather an act of aggression by a terrorist organization against a vulnerable population. After the Israelis seized the Negev desert, though, the Egyptians changed their minds and negotiated for peace on February 24, 1949. In return for the withdrawal of Egyptian troops and a pledge of non-aggression, Gaza would become a part of Egypt. Two months later, **Jordan** signed an armistice agreement which granted the West Bank (including Eastern Jerusalem) to the Hashemite Kingdom of Jordan under **Abdullah** in exchange for peace and possession of a few Arab villages in the central part of the state. **Syria** and **Lebanon** also signed peace agreements the same year.

In the end, the State of Israel encompassed 77% of Palestine, Egypt had its portion in the Gaza Strip and Jordan occupied East Jerusalem and the West Bank. The Palestinians, however, never saw the Palestinian Arab state envisioned by the **U.N. partition plan of 1947** (**U.N. Resolution 181**) and more than 800,000 Palestinians had become refugees in the course of the war.

Refugees
The first Palestinian exodus began after the announcement of the U.N. partition resolution when Arabs anticipating war temporarily relocated to neighboring countries. After word spread that on April 9, 1948 hundreds of innocent men, women and children were massacred by Jewish terrorists at **Deir Yassim**

(a small strategic village near Jerusalem) masses of Palestinians fled fearing the same fate would befall them. Others feared that they would be caught in the crossfire or become the victims of Jewish retaliation after the Arabs left. In some cases, Palestinian inhabitants were encouraged or ordered to leave either by the British, the Jews or the Arabs for their own safety or for strategic reasons (for example Arabs hoped to paralyze a city by evacuating all its workers). Finally, some Palestinians feared that if they remained in their isolated villages, they would be soon be surrounded by enemies or be regarded as traitors if they accepted Jewish protection.

Most of the refugees left their belongings behind believing that they would soon return after the fighting had stopped and the combined Arab forces had defeated the Zionists as they had promised. Expecting a speedy homecoming, wealthy Palestinians checked into hotels, took out short-term leases on apartments or visited relatives abroad. The majority, though, took up residence in tent cities just outside Israel's borders.

Since the camps were initially built as temporary shelters most lacked basic facilities such as running water, waste management, schools etc. Emergency assistance was provided by international organizations such as the International Red Cross and the American Friends Service Committee and in November 1948, the United Nations established the **United Nations Relief for Palestinian Refugees** (UNRPR) to help coordinate non-governmental relief organizations (NGOs).

When it became apparent that a swift return was not forthcoming, the UNRPR was replaced by the **United Nations Relief and Works Agency** (UNRWA) which set up more permanent services. Far from temporary, the UNRWA has been renewed every three years since its establishment in December 1949 and is expected to continue to serve the Palestinian refugees and their descendants as long as they are living in exile.

Resolution 194
According to UN General Assembly Resolution 194 issued in December 1948 (called the "**Right of Return**") Israel was instructed to "allow refugees to return to their homes at the earliest practical date to live in peace with their neighbors." Those who chose not to return or whose property was lost or damaged in the war, moreover, were entitled to compensation by the Israeli government..

But the mass exodus of Palestinians had served the Israelis well as they worked to accommodate an equally large influx of Jewish immigrants eager to settle in their new "homeland." Jews traumatized by the Holocaust in Europe readily took advantage of the new Israeli parliament's (Knesset) grant of immediate citizenship to any Jew who wanted to live in Israel (called the "**Law of Return**"). Others immigrated to Israel to avoid discrimination in Arab countries that bitterly opposed the Zionist occupation of Palestine. The number of Jewish immigrants, consequently, almost matched the number of Arabs who had fled hence permanently complicating any plans to repatriate the Palestinians (see "Refugees").

THE MIDDLE EAST AFTER WORLD WAR II

Transjordan

In fulfillment of the **MacMahon-Hussein** agreement which offered the Hashemite family authority over the Arab sections of the Ottoman Empire in return for Arab support in World War I, one of Sherif Hussein's sons, **Abdullah**, was installed as King over the new territory of Transjordan. Transjordan had been created by the British on the east bank of the Jordan River in 1921.

The appointment of a friendly Saudi prince in the Arab territory helped the British maintain a strong influence over the land route between the Mediterranean Sea and the Persian Gulf. As a Saudi national ruling a non-Saudi constituency Abdullah was dependent on Britain's support to uphold the legitimacy of his rule. The desperately poor nation was also dependent on the West for financial support.

Before the 1948 war, Transjordan had a fairly homogenous population that enthusiastically accepted Abdullah's rule. After the annexation of the West Bank of the Jordan River after 1948, though, the situation changed. Along with the territory, Jordan incorporated nearly half a million of the area's Palestinian inhabitants, most impoverished and many opposed to Hashemite rule because of the family's association with the hated British.

The annexation of the eastern half of Jerusalem (which included the Old City and the Noble Sanctuary/Temple Mount) into the Hashemite Kingdom of Jordan (as Transjordan was renamed) was also deeply resented by the Jews who were no longer permitted to visit their holy sites.

Despite the friction over Jerusalem, Abdullah maintained relatively good relations with Israel which led some Palestinian extremists to fear that he would make a separate peace with the Jewish nation. On July 21, 1951, Abdullah was assassinated on the steps of the Al Aqsa Mosque by one of these extremists.

He was succeeded briefly by his mentally unstable son, **Talal** who was then replaced by Abdullah's capable grandson, **Hussein**, who reigned over Jordan from 1952 until his death in 1999.

Tensions between the Jordanian leadership and the Palestinian refugee population continued to escalate until King Hussein was forced to expel the Palestinian Liberation Organization in 1970 (See "Black September.")

Syria

Historically "Syria" included Jordan, Israel, Lebanon as well as modern-day Syria. But because of its strategic location between the Mediterranean Sea and the Eastern deserts, the land was almost continuously dominated by greater powers hoping to take control of the important Middle East corridor.

For a while, Syria enjoyed a "golden age" under the rule of the *caliph* **Mu'awiya**

who declared the city of Damascus the capital of his glorious **Umayyad Dynasty** in A.D. 661. With the arrival of the **Abbasids** 100 years later, though, the center of the Muslim World was shifted east to Baghdad and Syria's wealth and prestige diminished accordingly. Under Turkish Ottoman domination (as the *Sanjak* of Damascus) Syria's status did not improve.

In the 20th century, the country's fortunes appeared to have turned after the famous British officer T.E. Lawrence and his band of Arabian rebels heroically rode into Damascus in 1918. For the next two years, Syria was ruled as an independent state by Sherif Hussein's son **Faisal**. As military governor, Faisal convened a General Congress and immediately began to reconstruct the country in Arabian fashion. The Congress declared Syria sovereign and free and, in March 1920, proclaimed Faisal the King of Syria. But independence was short-lived.

A month after the Allied Council meeting in San Remo confirmed the terms of the Sykes-Picot agreement, French soldiers marched from Beirut to Damascus to claim the mandate territory that had been granted to them by the Sykes Picot agreement. Faisal was forced out of the country and didn't return to the Middle East until the British made him the King of Iraq in 1921.

To solidify their rule in Syria, the French made the franc the basic unit of currency, enforced French as the compulsory language in schools, took control of banking institutions and divided the state into sectarian units.

After a series of local rebellions against them, the French were finally pressured by the United Nations into withdrawing from the area. On April 17, 1946, Syria officially became independent.

Once the French had left, though, Syria fell into a state of internal disorder with various sectors of society fighting among themselves over commercial, religious and political issues. The government had been rendered virtually ineffective by the quick turnover of leaders who illegally seized power in coups against the state. Only the **Ba'athists,** a party with pan-Arab, anti-West tendencies, were able to unite the population when they took over the country in 1954.

The Ba'athists were particularly popular among Syrians who harbored deep anti-Western sentiments due to their disappointment over the outcome of the **Versailles Peace Treaty** (see "World War I"), resentment over French occupation of the country, and anger over the West's defense of the state of Israel. As an alternative to the West, Syrians turned to the Soviet Union for aid and relied on camaraderie in the greater Arab community.

In 1956, consequently, the Syrian Ba'ath party joined the **Nasserists** of Egypt in an effort to create a **United Arab Republic**. Although the alliance disintegrated because of Syrian resentment over Egyptian domination, the dream of creating a pan-Arab nation persisted as did the hope that Greater Syria would once again be integrated into a state powerful enough to challenge the West.

Palestine in a Nutshell

Lebanon

In ancient times, the areas of Lebanon, Syria and Palestine, were inhabited by the Canaanites who founded the maritime empire of Phoenicia roughly within the borders of present-day Lebanon. The region had become Christian under Roman rule and, unlike Syria and Palestine, most of the people living in the area that eventually became Lebanon remained faithful to the **Maronite Christian Church** even after the Muslims conquered the area in the 7th century.

In the 11th century a Muslim sect called the **Druze** (followers of Fatimid *caliph* al-Hakim) settled in southern Lebanon and periodically quarreled with their Christian neighbors.

Under the Ottomans, the Lebanese enjoyed considerable autonomy and the Maronites, like other Catholic *millets* (religious minority communities) throughout the empire, were protected by the French who came to their aid in times of conflict. T,he Maronites frequently clashed with the Muslim Druze who, for their part were supported by the British.

When the French won administrative control over Syria (which included the area of Lebanon) after World War I, they separated the Catholic state of Lebanon from the Muslim territory of Syria and enlarged *le Grand Liban* (as they called it) beyond the borders that had been assigned to the territory in the old Ottoman *sanjak* of Lebanon.

Lebanon became an independent state in 1944 and joined the United Nations the next year. To accommodate the mixed population the government of Lebanon was shared by representatives of the various religious groups. As a rule, the President of Lebanon was a Maronite Christian, the Prime Minister a Sunni Muslim and the speaker of the National Assembly a Shia Muslim. The Christians, however, have traditionally dominated the country politically and economically.

Differences between the Christian and Muslim Lebanese eventually erupted into a civil war in 1975 which pitted the Christians (organized into the **Phalange** party), with U.S. and Israeli support, against the Muslims backed by the Palestinian Liberation Organization (PLO). The war lasted until 1990 and left the country in ruins.

Egypt

In 1859, a French company backed by British investors began digging a 100-mile canal in Egypt that connected the Mediterranean Sea and the Red Sea. Until then, ships bound from Europe to Asia were forced to navigate around Africa's Cape of Good Hope.

The opening of the Suez Canal ten years later was highly celebrated -- especially by the British who needed the waterway to get to their Indian colony in a fraction of the time -- and marked the beginning of British domination of Egyptian affairs.

At the start of World War I, Egypt formally became a British protectorate and when Egypt was granted titular independence from the Ottoman Empire in

1922, the country's new **King Fuad** and his son and successor **Farouk** were essentially British puppets.

In 1948, the Egyptians joined Syria, Transjordan, Lebanon and other Arab powers in the war against the newly-proclaimed state of Israel and agreed to a ceasefire a year later in exchange for control over the Gaza Strip.

The battle with Israel and growing corruption in the hated British-backed Farouk government stirred Egyptian nationalist sentiments and provoked hostility against the British presence.

In a bloodless coup in July 1952, consequently, King Farouk's unpopular puppet-regime was overthrown by a group of young officers led by **Lieutenant-Colonel Gamal Abdul Nasser**. Two years later, Nasser was declared President and became one of the most influential men in the Middle East in modern history.

As president, Nasser stoked Egypt's confrontation with Israel by building a military arsenal with aid from the Soviet Union[27] and supporting Palestinian guerrillas (*fedayeen*) in their raids against Israel from bases across the Israeli border.

His nationalist reforms were extremely popular within Egypt and his pan-Arab stance attracted devotees from around the Arab world positioning Egypt as the potential center for a greater Arab nation.

One of Nasser's boldest acts as president was the nationalization of the **Suez Canal** in July 1956 in order to generate revenues to fund his **Aswan Dam** project.. The move was a last resort after extensive efforts were made to secure foreign capital for the project but was perceived in the West as a deliberate provocation against the European powers.

In retaliation, British and French forces joined secretly with the Israelis (who were aggravated by Egypt's support of *fedayeen* raids) and attacked Egypt on October 29, 1956 (see "Sinai Campaign" in Israel section).

The combined British, French and Israeli armies were forced to withdraw by the United Nations who installed peace-keeping forces (the **UNEF** or **United Nations Emergency Forces**) along the Suez Canal and the Straits of Tiran (the shipping route from the Gulf of Aqaba to the Red Sea). Nasser's popularity soared when he was credited as the leader who had faced down the West and Israel.

The state of affairs in Egypt after the 1956 Suez War sowed the seeds for the 1967 Six-Day War.

---

[27] At the height of the Cold War between the U.S. and the Soviet Union, American President Eisenhower issued a doctrine that promised that the United States would provide economic and military aid to any country in the region that asked for protection from a communist-backed regime. The Arabs took advantage of the doctrine by accepting aid from one or the other superpower. In general, Egypt and Jordan accepted aid from the Soviets while Jordan and Israel were allied with Britain, France and the U.S.

Palestine in a Nutshell

PALESTINE LIBERATION ORGANIZATION (PLO)

As a consequence of the 1948 war, hundreds of thousands of Palestinians were living as refugees along the border of the newly proclaimed state of Israel. As "temporary" shelters, the camps that had been set up to accommodate the exiles lacked proper sewage, electricity, medical facilities, schools and other amenities and became a breeding ground of discontent among a destitute population that had been deprived of a homeland.

Initially, the camps received funding from their host countries (Jordan, Lebanon, Syria, Egypt etc.) but with their limited resources, the Arab countries could not bear the burden for very long [28] – nor could they afford to integrate the refugees into their own societies. In most of their host countries, therefore, the Palestinians were treated as foreigners whose movements and activities were restricted and opportunities limited. Even in the most accommodating countries (like Jordan where Palestinians were granted citizenship and the right to work) Palestinians were treated with suspicion and distrust.

The collective experience of displacement, frustration and anger bonded the Palestinians into a strong community with common aspirations and a unique identity. The struggle to reclaim Palestine was iterated on a regular basis by the exchange of the promise that "We shall return"[29] and the pursuit of self-determination colored nearly all activities within the camps.

Egypt's successful liberation from British tyranny and Nasser's nationalist ideals reinforced the Palestinians' claims of entitlement to a Palestinian homeland and encouraged the refugees to seek change through political means. The 1957 victory of the pan-Arab coalition of Egypt, Syria and the Palestinians against the British, French and Israelis in Sinai, furthermore, encouraged the Palestinians to band together militarily.

One year after the war, **Yasser Arafat**, a young Palestinian soldier who had fought with the Egyptians in the Suez campaign, joined some fellow students to form an underground movement dedicated to reclaiming Palestine. The organization, called **al-Fatah (Fatah)**, established training camps and bases in several Arab countries and launched its first operation on January 1st, 1965.

About the same time that Fatah was developing, Egyptian President Gamal Abdul Nasser called an Arab summit meeting in Cairo, Egypt, to discuss Israel's plans to divert water from the Jordan River to the Negev desert in order to supply new settlers in the territory. Although the water issue wasn't resolved, the attendees agreed to establish an institution that would represent the Palestinians now living in diaspora (*mahajir*). In 1964 the Palestinian Liberation Organization was born under the leadership of **Ahmed Shukairy**, a former Saudi ambassador to the U.N.

The aims and beliefs of the PLO were outlined in the 33 Articles of the **Palestinian National Charter of 1968**, excerpts of which follow:

Article 1: Palestine is the homeland of the Arab Palestinian people

---

[28] In 1950, the UNRWA assumed relief operations.

[29] The Jews in the Babylonian captivity repeated similar slogans with regard to Jerusalem.

42

Article 3: The Palestinian Arab people possess the legal right to their homeland

Article 4: The Palestinian identity is a genuine, essential and inherent characteristic.

Article 7: It is a national duty to bring up individual Palestinians in an Arab revolutionary manner. A Palestinian must be prepared for the armed struggle and ready to sacrifice his wealth and his life in order to win back his homeland and bring about its liberation.

Article 8: The phase of history though which the Palestinian people are now living is that of national struggle for the liberation of Palestine. [All other conflicts among the Palestinians are secondary].

Article 9: Armed struggle is the only way to liberate Palestine.

Article 10: Commando action constitutes the nucleus of the Palestinian popular liberation war.

Article 12: The Palestinians believe in Arab unity.

Article 13: Arab unity and the liberation of Palestine are two complementary objectives, the attainment of either of which facilitates the attainment of the other.

Article 14: The destiny of the Arab nation, and indeed Arab existence itself, depend upon the destiny of the Palestine cause.

Article 15: The liberation of Palestine, from an Arab viewpoint, is a national duty and it attempts to repel the Zionist and imperialist aggression against the Arab homeland and aims at the elimination of Zionism in Palestine.[30] Accordingly, the Arab nation must mobilize all its military, human, moral and spiritual capabilities to participate actively with the Palestinian people in the liberation of Palestine. [Arabs must also provide material and personnel in times of armed struggle.]

Article 16: The liberation of Palestine will provide the Holy Land with an atmosphere of safety and tranquility which in turn will safeguard the country's religious sanctuaries and guarantee freedom of worship and of visit to all, without discrimination of race, color, language or religion.

Article 19: The partition of Palestine in 1947 and the establishment of the state of Israel are entirely illegal because they were contrary to the will of the Palestinian people and to their natural right in their homeland and inconsistent with the principles embodies in the charter of the United Nations, particularly the right to self-determination.

Article 20: The Balfour Declaration, the Mandate for Palestine and everything that has been based upon them are deemed null and void. Claims of historical or religious ties of Jews with Palestine are incompatible with the facts of history and the true conception of what constitutes statehood. Judaism, being a religion is not an independent nationality.

---

[30] This and other references to Israel have been interpreted as a call for the "destruction of Israel."

Palestine in a Nutshell

Article 21: The Arab Palestinian people reject all solutions which are substitutes of the total liberation of Palestine.

Article 22: Zionism is racist and fanatic in its nature, aggressive, expansionist and colonial in its aims and fascist in its methods. Israel is the instrument of the Zionist movement and geographical base for world imperialism placed strategically in the midst of the Arab homeland to combat the hopes of the Arab nation for liberation, unity and progress. Israel is a constant source of threat vis-à-vis peace in the Middle East and the whole world.

***

In addition to negating the right of Israel to exist, the charter emphasized the connection between peace and unity among Arab countries in the Middle East and the liberation of Palestine and encouraged armed struggle to accomplish this goal. All Arab countries were expected to assist in this struggle for the total liberation of Palestine.

Initially, the younger members of the Fatah organization were wary of the PLO (which was sponsored by Egypt and attracted an older generation) and feared that it would be used by the Arab regimes to fulfill their own political agendas. But when it became apparent that the Fatah movement lacked the funds it needed to conduct effective attacks on Israel and the PLO (which had been discredited by its performance in the Six-Day War [See "Six-Day War"]) lacked Fatah's legitimacy, the organizations joined together.

The PLO eventually became the umbrella organization for a number of Palestinian groups (the Fatah movement being the dominant power in military and political affairs) and established training camps and centers all over the Arab world.

In 1968, the Palestine Liberation Organization won its first and most significant victory against Israeli armed forces at **al-Karameh**. On March 21, 1968, Israeli armored forces crossed the Jordan River to attack the Jordanian village of Karameh. With Jordan's blessing and support, Palestinian guerrilla fighters successfully repelled the Israelis.

The battle demonstrated that the Palestinian problem was not simply a humanitarian issue but a political issue as well. Although Palestinian casualties far outnumbered those of the Israelis, within the Arab community the victory was a psychological boost that attracted thousands of volunteer Palestinian fighters to the cause.

The guerrillas also enjoyed a new degree of respect and legitimacy which allowed them to operate freely in Jordan (up to then their movements were restricted) and won them international sympathy and support (including support from the Soviet Union). Within a decade, the United Nations General Assembly reaffirmed the inalienable rights of the Palestinian people to self-determination, national independence and sovereignty and the right of the Palestinians to return to their homes and property.[31]

In 1969, Yasser Arafat was elected Chairman of the Executive Committee of the PLO.

31 U.N. Resolution 3236 (XXIX), 1974

SIX-DAY WAR 1967

In 1964, the Egyptians called an Arab summit to discuss Israel's plans to divert water from the Sea of Galilee and the Jordan River to irrigate settlements in the Negev desert. At the time, the Arabs decided that they were not yet ready to fight a war with the Israelis over the issue. Instead they planned to divert water from the the river's tributaries into Syria and Lebanon. The Israelis responded by bombing the diversion works.

The Syrians, meanwhile, had been challenging Israel's increased use of land for agriculture in the demilitarized zones that had been set up along the border of Israel and Syria as part of the armistice agreement of 1949. The conflict between Syria and Israel escalated in 1966 when Syrians (under the rule of the more militant Ba'ath party) began to launch attacks on villages and Israeli farmers cultivating land in the demilitarized zone (DMZ) from bases in the Golan Heights high above the border areas.

When the Israelis retaliated on April 7, 1967, by shooting down six Soviet-supplied Syrian MiG fighter planes, the Syrians asked Egypt for help.

Egypt had been looking for an excuse to get rid of the U.N. Emergency forces (**UNEF**) that had been set up in strategic parts of the country since the 1956 Suez war and welcomed Syria's desire to strike up an alliance between the two Arab countries (Egypt and Syria had been at odds since the United Arab Republic alliance broke down in 1956). On May 15, 1967, two days after false reports were received from the Soviets that Israel was preparing for war against Syria, the Egyptians amassed troops near Israel's border. A day later, Egypt ordered all the U.N. forces to withdraw from their positions in the Sinai, along the Straits of Tiran and the Suez Canal. Once the UNEF had evacuated, the Egyptian navy blocked the Straits of Tiran preventing the passage of any Israeli vessels.[32]

By May 30, 1967, Jordan[33] had joined the Egyptian-Syrian alliance in preparation for war with Israel and Iraq joined a few days later. With hostile Arab forces surrounding the country, the Israelis took action.

On June 5, 1967, Israel launched the first strike by attacking Egypt's Air Force. While the Egyptian pilots were eating breakfast, the Israelis destroyed 309 of 340 combat airplanes on the ground rendering Egypt's air power useless. The Israeli Air Force then headed east to battle Jordanian forces which had begun to launch attacks in Jerusalem. The Jordanians were swiftly defeated due to Israel's air superiority. In the north, Israeli troops under the command of Defense

---

[32] The closure of the Straits of Tiran blocked Israel's only supply route with Asia and stopped the flow of oil from its main supplier, Iran.

[33] Jordan's King Hussein had been reluctant to move against Israel since friendly relations with the Jewish country helped him keep open valuable diplomatic channels to the British and Americans. If Hussein didn't support the war effort, though, he would have been considered a traitor in the eyes of the Arab world and the large population of Palestinians living within Jordanian borders

1967
Six Day War

Minister **Moshe Dayan** fought the determined Syrians until they were driven out of the Golan Heights.

Within six days the Israelis had successfully repelled the Arab forces and were making their way to Damascus, Amman and Cairo. With their capitals in imminent danger, the Arab allies were forced to retreat leaving Israel in control of Jordan's West Bank, Egypt's Gaza Strip and Sinai Peninsula and Syria's Golan Heights. The conquest caused another wave of Palestinian migration out of the area (some families moving for the second time after 1948) aggravating the already grave refugee crisis.

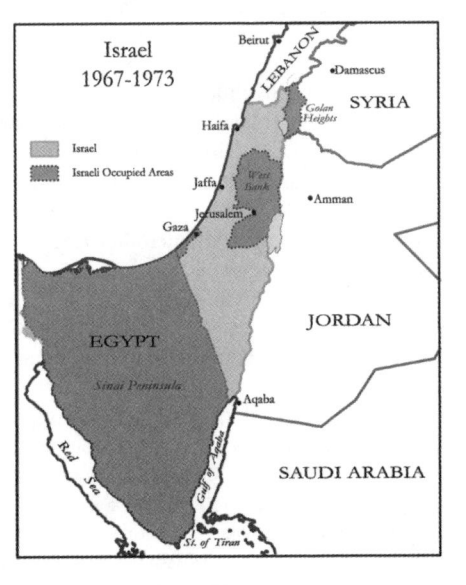

The war had also established Israel's military supremacy in the Middle East and the victory had been accomplished without the help of western allies. Without the assurance of western military support in future conflicts, however, the Israelis became more determined than ever to use military force to defend their borders. To solidify their authority (and in defiance of international law), the Israelis quickly moved hundreds of thousands of Jewish citizens into settlements built in the newly-won Arab territories.

For the Palestinians, the Arab defeat demonstrated that they could no longer rely on their Arab brothers to help them win back their homes. From that point on, the Palestinians became more organized militarily and politically and began to act independently of their Arab sponsors. The PLO, which up to then had been an Egyptian puppet organization, was taken over by younger, more militant Palestinians under the command of Yasser Arafat (who was made the PLO chairman a year after the Karameh victory of 1968) and turned to more aggressive tactics to win back land from the Israelis.

PFLP

Yasser Arafat's guerrilla organization, **Fatah**, was by far the largest guerrilla group conducting armed combat against Israel but there were others who didn't share Arafat's ideology.

In December, 1967, another organization called the **Popular Front for the Liberation of Palestine (PFLP)** was formed by **Dr. George Habash**, a Christian Palestinian. The organization was an outgrowth of the Arab Nationalist Movement that had been founded in Beirut in 1949 and had relied on Nasser's military strategies to promote its cause. After the Arab defeat in the Six-Day War, however, the PFLP, like other Palestinian groups, turned to revolutionary guerrilla activity.

Unlike Fatah, the PFLP maintained a Marxist-Leninist ideology and saw the liberation of Palestine as part of a greater goal to generate a worldwide Communist revolution. To that end, the PFLP made alliances with communist forces around the world -- especially the Soviet Union and China from where the organizations received most of its funding.

PFLP also theorized that the Palestinian struggle against Israel should be pursued by every possible means, including hijacking planes and acts of terror – anything that would harm Israel's interests. On July 23, 1968, the PFLP conducted its first hijacking by forcing an El Al airliner on its way to Tel Aviv from Rome to land in Algeria. A month later, the organization attacked an Israeli plane at Athens airport and, in 1970, the PFLP hijacked four Western jetliners and redirected them to Dawson Field, an airport near Amman, Jordan (where the PLO was then based).

By September 1970, the PFLP's radical activities (along with the organization's call for Palestinian control in Jordan) compelled **King Hussein** to drive all guerrilla groups out of the country in a deadly conflict called "**Black September**" by the Palestinians.

The hijacking operations were also criticized by Fatah, widening the rift that had already developed between the two organizations.

The PFLP formally broke with the PLO in 1993 to protest the **Oslo accords** (see "Peace Treaties" in Israel section) which it felt sold out the Palestinian refugees. Although the PFLP leaders and Arafat, leader of both Fatah and the PLO, reconciled six years later, the organizations maintained different views and took different approaches toward the Palestinian-Israeli problem. While Arafat publicly denounced terrorism, the PFLP continued to conduct small scale suicide bombings around Israel.

In 2000, Dr. Habash retired as the head of PFLP and was replaced by his extremist protégé, **Abu Ali Mustafa**. Mustafa moved his headquarters from Damascus (where the organization had been stationed after its expulsion from

Jordan) to the city of Ramallah and resumed the military struggle against Israel (regardless of Arafat's pledges of non-violence at Oslo seven years earlier). Only a year after he was made the PFLP's General Secretary, Mustafa was assassinated by the Israeli Army.

In retaliation for the murder, Mustafa's successor **Ahmed Sadat** became the first Palestinian to order the assassination of an Israeli minister. In October 2001, the PFLP escalated Israeli-Palestinian violence by killing Israel's rightist Tourism Minister **Rechavan Ze'evi**. In January 2002, Sadat was arrested for his role in the Ze'evi assassination.

The PFLP had set the stage for a number of radical organizations including **Hamas** and **Islamic Jihad** but was not very prominent itself. Only about 3% of Palestinians supported PFLP while Fatah and other Islamist groups such as Hamas each commanded support of more than 30% of the Palestinian population.

Like other organizations that relied on economic support from the Soviet Union, the PFLP suffered financially after the collapse of the USSR.

DFLP or PDFLP (Popular Democratic Front for the Liberation of Palestine)

In 1969, the extreme revolutionary, **Nayif Hawatmeh** (a Jordanian Christian), split from the PLFP to form the Democratic Front for the Liberation of Palestine. The DFLP adopted a purer Marxist-Leninist doctrine believing that Palestinian goals could only be achieved through revolution of the masses. In 1974, the DFLP was the first organization to propose the creation of a democratic "**national authority**" in the West Bank and Gaza as opposed to total liberation of Palestine. This concept became the basis for Arafat's declaration at the Palestine National Congress meeting in 1988 when he stated that the Palestinian leadership was willing to consider the division of historic Palestine into two states (Israel and Palestine).

PFLP – General Command (PFLP – GC)

The Popular Front for the Liberation of Palestine – General Command was formed in 1968 by former PFLP leader **Ahmed Jibril**. The PFLP – GC declared it wanted to focus more on fighting and less on politics and in 1974 it claimed responsibility for the first suicide bombings by Palestinians. The PFLP was violently opposed to Yasser Arafat's PLO.

Palestine Liberation Front (PLF)

The Palestine Liberation Front, headed by **Muhammad Zaidan (Abu Abbas)** and **Tal'at Ya'akub**, broke away from the PFLP-GC in 1977. In the 1990s the PLF accepted the PLO's policy of halting terrorist activity as outlined in the Oslo agreement. Prior to that, the organization was best known for its 1985 attack on the Italian cruise ship Achille Lauro during which a wheelchair-bound American Jew was tossed overboard. Abu Abbas was arrested in Iraq in April 2003 for the ship's hijacking -- though his arrest was challenged by the PLO because the attack had taken place before September 13, 1993, the day the Oslo accord was signed.

BLACK SEPTEMBER

After the 1967 Six-Day War another flood of Palestinian refugees left the West Bank, Gaza Strip and Golan Heights as the territories fell into Israeli hands. Most of the refugees joined their comrades in Jordan's east bank of the Jordan River where the PLO, which had become radicalized after the Arab defeat, had set up its headquarters.

At least seven Palestinian guerrilla organizations were now stationed in Jordan, each embracing different ideologies and each engaging different tactics to accomplish the goal of reclaiming the Palestinian state.

In the beginning the Jordanians under **King Hussein** supported the Palestinian struggle by providing training sites and assistance. As the guerrilla groups became wealthier (through funding from other Arab states and the Soviet Empire), and more emboldened (particularly after the successful **Karameh** battle), they began to openly flout Jordanian law and challenge King Hussein's authority. The Palestinians had become a virtual state-within-a-state whose agenda had shifted from returning to their homeland to expanding their power in exile at the expense of the Jordanian government.

The Israelis, meanwhile, launched attacks on a number of Jordanian cities in retaliation for the Karameh conflict and in response to guerrilla activity staged in Jordan against Israeli targets.

In June 1970, King Hussein tried to stabilize the growing animosity between his government and the *fedayeen* (Palestinian fighters) by drawing up a conciliatory agreement. The agreement stated that the Jordanian government would allow commandos to move freely within Jordan and refrain from anti-guerrilla action in return for a *fedayeen* pledge to remove bases from Amman and other major cities and show respect for Jordanian law. The peace plan was soon violated by both parties.

In spite of the agreement, the *fedayeen* called a general strike and continued to organize civil disobedience campaigns. In the same year, the PFLP openly defied Jordanian authority by hijacking foreign planes and forcing them to land in Jordan. Another airliner was flown to the Cairo airport and blown up in front of TV cameras minutes after passengers and crew had been evacuated.

In response, in September, 1970, King Hussein declared martial law and ordered the *fedayeen* to lay down their arms and evacuate Jordanian cities. For the next ten days, ("Black September" to the Palestinians), the Jordanian Arab Army and the **Palestinian Liberation Army** (the military branch of the PLO), fought a deadly civil war that drew in the United States Navy (supporting the Jordanians) and Syrian forces (supporting the Palestinians). The Israelis were also standing by to deploy aid to King Hussein if needed.

By the time a cease-fire was declared on September 25, more than 3,000 people had been killed. After the war, prisoners were released from both sides and the guerrilla forces retreated to positions along the border where they could continue their battle with Israel . The *fedayeen* had also agreed to recognized Jordanian sovereignty and the King's authority in return for amnesty for crimes committed during the war.

Palestine in a Nutshell

Towards the end of 1970 and the beginning of 1971 skirmishes started up again between the two groups as the Jordanians pressured the *fedayeen* to withdraw from major cities. King Hussein finally ordered his minister, **Wasfi al Tal**, to decisively deal with Palestinian plotters who wanted to establish a separate Palestinian state within Jordan. Guerrilla bases in northern Jordan were destroyed and thousands of *fedayeen* were arrested. Most of the Palestinian prisoners were released a few days later with two choices: either peacefully re-enter into Jordanian life or relocate. By the end of 1971, the PLO had moved its headquarters to Lebanon.

In November of the same year, Hussein's Prime Minister, Tal, was assassinated by a new Palestinian extremist group called the "**Black September**" (named after the month in which the civil war had occurred) to avenge the death of fellow Palestinians.

LEBANON WAR

Long before the creation of Israel and the subsequent arrival of more than 100,000 Palestinian refugees, Lebanon maintained a delicate ethnic-religious balance between Christians (Maronites, Greek Orthodox, Armenian Orthodox and Catholic) and Muslims (Druze, Sunni and Shi'ites). In order to ensure that all groups were represented fairly, government posts were apportioned to each of the religious groups. For example, a **Maronite** served as president, the prime minister was **Sunni** and a **Shiite** served as the speaker of the National Assembly. This fragile balance was disturbed, though, with the arrival of the **Palestine Liberation Organization** (PLO) after the organization had been expelled from Jordan in the early 1970s (see "Black September").

After the 1948 war, the Palestinians in Lebanon, like fellow refugees in other Arab countries, were housed in temporary **UNRWA** (U.N. Relief and Works Agency)-operated tent shelters that eventually gave way to single-story concrete houses (often lacking plumbing, sewage systems and other amenities). Over time, many of the refugees moved to surrounding districts but the camps remained at the core of Palestinian activity.

As temporary residents, the Palestinians were not granted the same legal rights as other Lebanese citizens and were denied access to state education, Lebanon's social welfare programs and other institutions. They were also prohibited from taking jobs in many skilled and professional occupations. Consequently, the refugees were forced to accept low paying jobs with few benefits which further perpetuating their substandard living conditions. Camp life and Palestinian movement, moreover, was tightly controlled by the Lebanese government and political activity was strictly prohibited in the 1950s and 60s.

After 1967, the situation changed as anti-Western and anti-Israeli feelings were fiercely aroused in the Muslim Lebanese community as a result of Israel's seizure of the West Bank, Gaza and the Golan Heights. By 1969 most Lebanese sympathized with the Palestinian struggle and supported the *fedayeen* in their operations against the Israelis across Lebanon's southern border.

Although some members of the Lebanese government (especially the Maronite Christian leaders) continued to insist that the Palestinian guerrillas did not belong in Lebanese territory, popular pressure compelled the government to issuing the **Cairo Agreement**. This 1969 accord (which was masterminded by Gamal Abdul Nasser of Egypt and signed by Yasser Arafat) granted the PLO the right to assume responsibility for managing the affairs of the Palestinian community in Lebanon and gave the guerrillas free reign over recruitment, training, weapon procurement and military activity staged there against the Israelis.

The same privileges were accorded to the masses of Palestinians who flooded to Palestinians refugee camps in Lebanon after they were driven out of Jordan in 1970-71. With the PLO headquarters now established in Beirut and Palestinian guerrillas controlling substantial portions of southern Lebanon, the PLO was able to create a state-within-a-state with social and economic institutions and government administration. In the camps, the Palestinians improved the supply of electricity and water, created a public sanitation system and built

hospitals and clinics that were open to Lebanese as well as Palestinians. In many ways, the Palestinians felt they were establishing a state infrastructure that would eventually be transferred to Palestine itself.

From their new base, the Palestinian guerrillas also stepped up attacks against the Israelis (and Americans[34]) which were countered by massive Israeli assaults against the Lebanese. The Israelis believed that by striking Lebanon in retaliation for allowing the Palestinians to operate from their borders, they would eventually encourage the Lebanese to suppress the guerrillas themselves. The tactic worked.

In order to put an end to the Israeli attacks, the Lebanese government called on the PLO to cease their activity. Unwilling to have a repeat of "Black September," in January 1972, the PLO agreed to temporarily curtail its activities in southern Lebanon. But the PLO leadership had difficulty convincing members of the individual guerrilla groups to abide by the unpopular suspension of military action. Recognition of such a freeze was seen as an abandonment of the PLO's commitment to conduct armed struggle against the Israelis until they were expelled from Palestine. Breaching the freeze, on the other hand, demonstrated a violating group's ardent commitment to the struggle over those who curtailed their militant activity. The most virulent militants, therefore, enjoyed the highest prestige and anti-Israeli activity continued despite the "official" suspension.

By 1972, relations between the Palestinians and Lebanese had deteriorated in large part because of persistent Israeli retaliatory attacks but also because of the great degree of Palestinian autonomy and the offensive conduct of some of the guerrillas. Provincial leaders felt their authority was being challenged by the self-governing Palestinians and the Lebanese community was indignant over the behavior of rogue Palestinian guerrillas who deliberately flouted Lebanese laws and harassed the populace.

Civil War
In 1975, the Palestinians became embroiled in a Lebanese civil war that pitted the Muslim majority, organized as the **Lebanese National Movement (LNM)**, against the ruling **Maronite Christians** and their **Phalangist** militia. The LNM wanted changes to be made in the Lebanese government to reflect their growing interests while the Maronites favored maintaining the status quo.

Along with the Palestinians, who sided with the Lebanese National Movement against the Maronites, the civil war attracted a number of participants from abroad who supplied both sides with vast quantities of arms. In April 1976, the Syrians began to intervene to prevent the country from being partitioned and the Israelis welcomed the war as a way to direct Palestinian and Syrian attention away from Israel and as an opportunity to establish friendly relations with the Christian Lebanese. The alliance allowed the Israelis to establish a pro-Israeli enclave in southern Lebanon under **Saad Haddad**, a Lebanese Christian officer.

---

[34] Guerrilla members of the PFLP conducted a number of attacks against American targets in Lebanon.

The Israeli presence became a full-scale invasion in 1978 in retaliation for a Palestinian bus hijacking north of Tel Aviv. In three days, the Israelis moved 20,000 Israeli troops up to the Litani River before they were forced to retreat by the United Nations. To monitor the withdrawal and restore international peace and security, the United Nations dispatched the **United Nations Interim Force in Lebanon** (**UNIFIL**) in southern Lebanon. The Israeli invasion posed a great challenge to the Palestinian leadership and the presence of U.N. peace-keeping forces frustrated their military aspirations.

The PLO by that time had grown from a loosely organized collection of guerrilla fighters to a vast bureaucratic network with a budget in the hundreds of millions of dollars and employing thousands of civil servants. The organization was able to support a number of social programs and provide assistance to Palestinians and Lebanese civilians who had suffered from Israeli attacks.

PLO military, economic and political strength in Lebanon was especially daunting to the Israelis who feared the organization could eventually win international recognition and pose a real political threat to the Israeli nation to prevent this from happening. The Israelis decided to inflict their final blow on the organization in 1982 after the Palestinians had lost their biggest ally, the Egyptians (who had signed a peace treaty with Israel in 1979) and while the PLOs popularity within Lebanon was low.

Using the attempted assassination of **Shlomo Argov**, Israel's ambassador in London, as a pretext (there had been no attacks on Israel for a year following an unofficial ceasefire arranged by the United Nations with American help), the Israelis launched another invasion of Lebanon in June 1982. This time, the majority of Lebanese Muslim and Druze militias and other Lebanese groups who had supported the Palestinians earlier did not fight alongside the PLO troops to resist the Israelis.

The Israeli army swept north flattening Palestinian camps and forcing PLO fighters to retreat further and further into Lebanon until they were surrounded in the western half of Beirut. For 67 days the Israelis laid siege to the city and its inhabitants until Arafat agreed to pull out of Beirut to prevent further civilian casualties.[35]

With the PLO gone, the remaining Palestinian community was deprived of all the services that had been provided by the organization. Even more distressing, the evacuation of PLO militiamen left the refugees vulnerable to attack. Just days after Multi-National Forces (MNF) withdrew from Palestinian areas, Lebanese Phalange Forces (seeking revenge for the assassination of one of their leaders) raided the **Sabra and Shatila refugee camps in** search of "terrorists." For the next two days, the Phalangists used their power to settle old scores by slaughtering more than a thousand Palestinian men, women and children and

---

[35] Israel maintained a military presence in Lebanon until they were required to withdraw their troops in fulfillment of U.N. **Security Council 425** in May 2000.

bulldozing their bodies into mass graves. The Israelis under then defense-minister **Ariel Sharon**, who had sanctioned the Phalangists entry into the camps, turned a blind eye to the massacre.[36]

In 1987, the Cairo Agreement was formally annulled and Palestinian refugees who continued to reside in Lebanon were relegated to second-class citizens lacking the legal rights enjoyed by other Lebanese citizens and subject to discriminatory restrictions.

The PLO, which relocated to Tunisia, suffered serious losses after the 1982 war. With its headquarters situated so far from the Israeli battlefield and its Palestinian constituents, the organization had trouble maintaining its authority and cohesion. Without its fighters recruited from the camps, moreover, the PLO's military strength waned.

In its place, a number of independent militant organizations sprang up (**Hezbollah**, **Hamas** and **Islamic Jihad** among them) espousing various agendas and exercising different degrees of violence to accomplish their goals. The Palestinians in the Occupied Areas, meanwhile, began to take matters into their own hands by staging a general uprising or *intifada*.

---

[36] In 2001, it was suggested by the BBC (British Broadcasting Corp.) that Ariel Sharon should be tried for war crimes because he "disregarded" the danger that the Phalangists might carry out acts of vengeance when he decided to let them enter the camps and by not taking appropriate measures to reduce the risk of a massacre.

INTIFADA

After the 1982 Lebanon War and the PLO's relocation to Tunis, Tunisia, the organization had lost much of its influence. The PLO's effectiveness plunged even further after the Israelis bombed the Tunis headquarters in 1985 and Jordan closed PLO offices in Amman and deported its top leader, **Khalil al-Wazir**.

Without the support of the diminished organization, Palestinians living within the Occupied Territories of Gaza and the West Bank were isolated in their struggle to survive much less battle with the Israelis.

Life in the refugee camps was grim, especially when compared to the living standards enjoyed by Israelis living in heavily guarded settlements built on Palestinian-populated land. The camps still lacked adequate sewage, electrical and water services, roads were still substandard, benefits were scarce and the camps were becoming increasingly congested.

Since 1948, the population of Palestinians living in exile had nearly doubled due to high fertility rates and better medical services. By the mid 1980s therefore, the camps were overrun with children and young adults who had grown up as refugees. As these young Palestinians came of age, moreover, they saw only bleak futures ahead of them.

The cycle of poverty among Palestinians was perpetuated by the underdevelopment of and limitations imposed on Palestinian industry and by the heavy restrictions put on camp residents who had no source of employment except in Israel. Once workers crossed the heavily guarded, time-consuming checkpoints set up between Palestinian areas and Israeli cities, they found their income opportunities limited to low-paying industrial and construction jobs with no benefits or job security.

Some Palestinians took advantage of the oil-boom from 1973 to 1982 and found employment in Arab oil-producing countries. When oil revenues shriveled in the mid-80s, though, the demand for expatriate workers in the Gulf fell dramatically forcing the Palestinians to return to the camps. The returning workers only added to camp overpopulation and the workers were forced to compete with other local Palestinians for jobs.

The Israelis also regulated and limited Palestinian industrial and agricultural ventures which competed with Israeli businesses. Permits were withheld from some expanding Palestinian companies, for example, and Palestinian farmers were prohibited from purchasing advanced machinery and were only permitted to grow and sell certain crops.

In 1985, Israel's defense minister **Yitzhak Rabin** further stoked the discontent by enacting **Iron Fist II**, a program that stepped up the presence and power of the Israeli military in the West Bank and Gaza strip and was designed to crush

Palestinian resistance. Rather than controlling the population, though, Iron Fist II only drove resistance underground and toughened the Palestinian resolve.

The simmering rage came to a head on December 8, 1987 as a group of Palestinian men were waiting to cross a checkpoint after a long day of low-paid work in Israel. That evening, an Israeli military vehicle swerved into a line of cars killing four Palestinians and wounding seven others. Although the crash was probably the result of faulty brakes, a rumor spread that the accident had been deliberate to avenge the earlier death of an Israeli soldier. The rumor, coupled with existing anger over the occupation and substandard living conditions, was enough to trigger a spontaneous demonstration at the funeral of the victims (attended by more than 6,000 Palestinians from all over Gaza).

The Israelis responded by using live ammunition, tear gas and beatings to try to disperse the demonstrators resulting in the death of a 20-year old Palestinian and many people being injured.

News of the funeral incident and the death of another Palestinian youth near Nablus, spread throughout the Palestinian community inspiring thousands of refugees to take to the streets.

The growing uprising (or *intifada* which means "shaking off" in Arabic) spread to other cities and villages in the occupied areas and began to attract Palestinians from all over Palestinian territories.

Within a month, the PLO (which had only learned about the *intifada* from newscasts) decided to capture the momentum of the popular uprising by coordinating its movements to guarantee the greatest results. The PLO created the **Unified National Leadership of the Uprising** (UNLU) to take on the responsibility. In its first directive, the new protest leaders called on all sectors of Palestinian society to support the strike by refusing to go to work, by closing businesses and by evading Israeli taxes and boycotting Israeli products. Those who didn't comply would be punished as traitors. Other Palestinians continued to fight back by erecting barricades and lobbing rocks, bricks and Molotov cocktails at Israeli forces.

In retaliation, more than 100,000 Israeli troops were deployed in the Gaza area to put down the rebellion. To disperse the demonstrators troops fired rubber bullets (and sometimes live ammunition) at unarmed refugees, sprayed them with teargas etc. Thousands of Palestinians were imprisoned in increasingly crowded jails and the Israelis punished entire villages for the uprising by cutting off their water, electricity or fuel supplies or slashing phone lines. Restrictive

---

37 Jordan paid the salaries of striking workers, for instance, and Iraq offered to pay pensions to the families of those who were disabled or killed during the fighting.

38 The two-state compromise was originally conceived in 1969 by the DFLP as a first step towards establishing a single secular democratic state where Palestinian natives (Christians and Muslims) could live in harmony with foreign Jewish settlers.

curfews were administered for days at a time and Palestinian merchants were sometimes forced to open their shop doors in defiance of strike-orders or risk having the doors welded shut or the shops destroyed.

The heavy-handed Israeli response to the uprising, meanwhile, was broadcast around the world. Images of Palestinian youths throwing rocks at heavily armed Israeli soldiers won international support for the Palestinians. Demonstrations of solidarity erupted internationally in sympathy with the Palestinian under-dogs and Arab leaders pledged financial and moral support to keep the *intifada* going.[37] The uprising brought new awareness to the Palestinian cause and affected the course of the PLO.

At the 19th session of the **Palestinian National Council** or **PNC** (the PLO executive committee) which convened in Algiers in November 1988, the Palestinian delegates voted to accept a "two-state" solution based on **U.N. Resolution 181.** The plan would partition the land into a Palestinian Authority (including the West Bank and Gaza Strip) and an Israeli sector.[38] Although the **Palestinian Authority** (PA) wasn't recognized abroad until 1994, the Palestinians in the occupied areas celebrated the November 14, 1988, "declaration of independence" with parades and celebrations.

With worldwide opinion behind him, Arafat presented the PLO's compromise at the U.N. General Assembly in Geneva on December 13, 1988. Along with the two-state solution and the pronouncement that the PLO formally recognized Israel's right to exist, Arafat publicly denounced terrorism and accepted territorial concessions in the name of peace.

Despite Arafat's conciliatory tone and international backing, though, Israeli leaders still refused to negotiate with the PLO deeming it a "terrorist organization." Instead the Israelis offered to grant Palestinians autonomy over civilian affairs without any mention of the PLO or an independent Palestinian state. The compromise was overwhelmingly rejected.

Arafat's declaration also drove a wedge between the PLO and the hard-line Palestinian groups who felt the organization was abandoning the struggle to restore Palestine to its rightful owners. The guerrilla organization **Hamas**, for instance, officially condemned "the calls for ending the *jihad* (holy war) and the establishment of peace with the murderers."

The *intifada* began to wane in 1990, a year before Arafat's fateful decision to back Saddam Hussein in his invasion of Kuwait during the Gulf War of 1991.

---

[37] Jordan paid the salaries of striking workers, for instance, and Iraq offered to pay pensions to the families of those who were disabled or killed during the fighting

[38] The two-state compromise was originally conceived in 1969 by the DFLP as a first step towards establishing a single secular democratic state where Palestinian natives (Christian and Muslim) could live in harmony with foreign Jewish settlers.

MILITANT ORGANIZATIONS

Hamas

In the midst of the fiery *intifada* grew an Islamic movement that was second only to Fatah in its influence and a serious competitor to the PLO.

Hamas (meaning "zeal" in Arabic and the acronym for Harakat al-Muqawama al-Islamiya or "Islamic Resistance Movement") was an offshoot of **Muslim Brotherhood (MB)**, an Egyptian organization with branches throughout the Arab world espousing Islamic ideals

Its leader, **Sheikh Ahmad Yassin** ran the Palestinian branch of the Muslim Brotherhood from its base in the Gaza Strip when Gaza was still part of Egypt. After the 1967 war and the incorporation of Gaza into Israel, Yassin continued to develop the social programs that were the cornerstone of the organization while emphasizing its Palestinian character and patriotism.

When the *intifada* began, the Palestinian Muslim Brotherhood changed its name to Hamas and helped fuel the uprising by distributing leaflets and encouraging insurgency. With its headquarters in Gaza, where Palestinian refugees experienced the worst socio-economic hardships, Hamas was able to build a large base of supporters. In contrast, the PLO based in remote Africa was distanced from the refugees they claimed to represent.

Also unlike the secular Palestinian Organization, Hamas members believed that Palestine was an Islamic *waqf* (property permanently set aside for religious purposes) that could not be divided or shared -- although, as a Muslim state, Christians, Jews and other religious minorities would be permitted to peacefully coexist with Muslims and practice their faiths freely.

In the battle to liberate Palestine from the Zionists and reestablish it as an Islamic state, Hamas advocated armed struggle and ultimately all-out *jihad* (holy war). Toward this end, Hamas trained and dispatched an army of "freedom fighters" or *mujaheddin* (holy warriors) who had been recruited to further the cause by targeting soft Israeli targets – in most cases by detonating explosives strapped to their bodies in public places. Those who died in the name of *jihad* were lauded in the community as martyrs who deserved a special place in heaven.[39] Families of the fallen "heroes" were also rewarded with large sums of money and honored by their Palestinian neighbors. The bombings, which resulted in the deaths of hundreds of Israeli civilians, earned Hamas a place in U.S. President **George Bush's** official list of terrorist groups in November 2001.

In addition to its military enterprises, Hamas devoted much of its annual budget to extensive social services. The **Islamic Charity** operated a network of schools, orphanages, health clinics and welfare programs – all sorely needed in

---

[39] Candidates for martyrdom believe that the first drop of blood that is shed in the name of Allah (God) washes away their sins allowing them to enter the highest level of heaven. In heaven, they are greeted by 72 *houris* (beautiful virgins). They are also allowed to select 70 of their nearest friends and family members to automatically enter heaven.

the squalid refugee camps. It also ran youth-league volleyball and soccer teams in the Gaza Strip and provided food and cash to impoverished Palestinians.

To fund these programs (which were not offered by the PLO or any other Palestinian groups), Hamas depended on financial aid from abroad. Pious Muslims observing one of the five requirements in Islam, the giving of charity or *zakat*, eagerly donated money to Hamas to pay for its humanitarian services and a broad network of charity associations were set up around the world to coordinate these financial transactions. Because of Hamas' charitable nature, a recent U.S. government decision to freeze the assets of Hamas leaders in response to Hamas-sponsored attacks in Israel was interpreted by some Muslims as an act against Islam.

Since its creation, Hamas has been accepted as an alternative organization to the PLO and has attracted a number of Palestinians who were drawn by the movement's benevolent works, emphasis on Islam and perceived dedication to the Palestinian cause.[40] The PLO, conversely, has been discredited by many Hamas supporters as a corrupt, secular institution that sold out to the Israelis and the Americans by participating in the peace process. Hamas leaders were violently opposed to the **Oslo Accords** of 1993 and other compromises with the Israelis which they viewed as furthering the Zionist goal to "expand from the Nile to the Euphrates."[41]

The popularity of Hamas and its condemnation of the peace process has put Arafat in a difficult position. On the one hand, if Arafat undertakes any measures to suppress Hamas activity he risks being accused by Palestinians of doing Israel's bidding and helping the Zionists undermine the opposition. On the other hand, any association between the PLO leader and the militant organization could derail the peace process (which was predicated on Arafat's promises to put an end to terrorism in Israel) and threaten his international role as mediator between the Palestinians and the Israelis. To avoid confrontation, therefore, Arafat has maintained a delicate balance between the two poles by simultaneously appeasing the West (by publicly denouncing violence and arresting Hamas leaders) and supporting the Palestinian cause (by releasing Hamas prisoners shortly after they are detained and praising the "martyrs" in Arabic).

Islamic Jihad
The name Islamic Jihad (Harakat al-Jihad al-Islami) has been used by a number of organizations inspired by Iran's 1979 Islamic Revolution and the rise of Islamic militancy in the Middle East in the 1970s and 80s. But the group begun by **Fathi Shaqaqi** (or Shqaqi, Shikaki) has been the most active and is the most recognized.

Shaqaqi was born in the Gaza Strip in 1951 and studied mathematics in the West Bank. In 1974, he studied medicine in Egypt where he became active in

---

[40] Arafat's Fatah organization and Hamas each command support from approximately 30% of the Palestinian population.

[41] As stated in the Hamas' Islamic Covenant published in August 1988.

the **Egyptian Muslim Brotherhood** (MB). He soon became embroiled in an ideological dispute with fellow members over the importance of Palestine in MB's pan-Islamic ambitions. While adherents of the Muslim Brotherhood believed that the unification of the Islamic world was a prerequisite for the liberation of Palestine, Shaqaqi and his followers saw the destruction of Israel as an essential first step towards the creation of a greater Islamic state.

The 1979 Iranian revolution, the rise of the **Ayatollah Khomeini** and the transformation of Iran into a purely Islamic state ruled by religious leaders further inspired Shaqaqi and other Muslims who saw the revolution as a model for the Arab world. Shaqaqi, in fact, was the first Sunni Muslim (the revolutionaries, as well as most Persians, were Shi'ite Muslims) to publish a book glorifying Khomeini and praising "The Islamic Solution."

Shaqaqi saw his fortunes in Egypt fade, however, after his book was banned (earning him three months in jail) and when Egyptian authorities expelled all Islamic radicals (Shaqaqi among them) after the assassination of Egyptian President **Anwar Sadat** in 1981.

Shaqaqi returned to Gaza where he organized a group of students to form the **Palestinian Islamic Jihad** (PIJ) committed to the creation of an Islamic Palestinian state and the destruction of Israel through holy war (*jihad*).

With funding from Iran's religious leaders, Islamic Jihad developed a military apparatus that carried out attacks against Israeli soldiers – the most notably being an assault on military recruits attending an induction meeting at the Wailing Wall in Jerusalem carried out by the organization in the 1980s.

In 1988, the group's leaders were expelled from Gaza after Shiqaqi was found smuggling arms into Gaza. A year later, in their new residences in Lebanon and then Syria (where Islamic Jihad now has its headquarters) the group came into direct contact with members of Hezbollah and their Persian benefactors. From their new bases, Islamic Jihad continued to conduct deadly attacks on Israeli targets with Iran as the movement's major financial supporter and Hezbollah providing it with training facilities and logistical aid.

In 1993, the formerly competitive Islamic Jihad and Hamas joined together in a Damascus-based **Alliance of Palestinian Forces** (APF) in opposition to the Oslo Accords which they considered a betrayal of Palestinian and Islamic rights.[42] To halt the peace process, the two organizations coordinated attacks that left dozens of Israelis dead.

After the assassination of Shiqaqi in October 1995, by unknown assailants, Islamic Jihad activities dropped dramatically leading Israel and the West to sur-

---

[42] Neither organization recognized the Arafat-led Palestinian Authority (created as a result of the Oslo Accords) as a legitimate government or participated in the 1996 Palestinian Authority elections.

mise that the murdered leader had been the driving force of the organization without whose leadership Islamic Jihad could not function.

With the eruption of the second *intifada* in 2000, though, the organization experienced a rebirth, in part because of increased funding from Iran [43] and also as a result of greater coordination with other Palestinian groups (including Hamas and radical Fatah members). In September of that year, Islamic Jihad's new leader **Ramadan Abdallah Shalah**[44] proclaimed "Our enemy possesses the most sophisticated weapons in the world and its army is trained to a very high standard... We have nothing with which to repel killing and thuggery against us except the weapons of martyrdom. It is easy and costs us only our lives...human bombs cannot be defeated, not even by nuclear bombs."

Despite its reputation and the magnitude of its destruction, Islamic Jihad has remained a small group lacking the popular support accorded to Hamas and the PLO.[45] Its small size, however, has allowed the organization to concentrate on its ideals and operate free of the constraints put on the larger Palestinian movements.

Martyrs/Freedom Fighters

Against an Israeli army of more than two million conscripts (including men and women) and a military budget that has reached nearly two billion dollars, the Palestinians couldn't compete in a traditional sense. Where Palestinians could gain a military advantage, though, was through their own method of warfare. Like the rag-tag guerrilla fighters in America fighting against trained and disciplined British troops during the American Revolution, Palestine's "Freedom Fighters" have learned to battle Israel in an unconventional manner with fewer funds, fewer troops and an element of surprise that, militants hoped, would eventually destabilize the Israeli behemoth to the point of collapse.

Already, the seemingly random attacks against Israeli civilians by "martyrs" loaded with explosives have triggered a slow exodus from the country and deterred investors and potential immigrants from moving into the country. [46] The assaults have also drawn international attention to the Palestinian plight and contributed to Israel's urgency to find a solution to the Israeli-Palestinian conflict.

The large-scale practice of using one's own body to fight a war or *jihad* was first exercised in Iran in the course of its war with Iraq. Hoping to break down Iraqi defenses, Iran sent massive numbers of unarmed or lightly armed elderly men, children and sometimes women as human "waves" against Iraq's better

---

[43] It is believed that Iran paid Islamic Jihad million-dollar bonuses for each attack against Israel.

[44] Before assuming the role of leader of Islamic Jihad after Shiqaqi's death in 1995, Shalah was a Florida professor educated in London, England.

[45] Only 4 to 5% of Palestinians support Islamic Jihad.

[46] In the first eight months of 2001, Israel received 28,212 new arrivals. In 2002, 21,303 immigrants entered the country in the first eight months but only 14,082 arrived in the first eight months of 2003 (source: Jewish Agency for Israel)

equipped forces. Thousands of willing "martyrs" were slaughtered with each assault as the Iranian government continued to send them to the front.

The selfless and pious devotion of these fighters inspired members of Islamic Jihad and Hamas (who received much of their aid from Iran) and other organizations that employed human bombs to accomplish political goals. These "martyrs" were not "committing suicide," it was reasoned, but were giving their most precious and valuable possession, their lives, to serve Allah (God). In the same context, Palestinian bombers were committing the same ultimate sacrifice for their people and God.

While "suicide" is strictly forbidden in the Muslim religion, those who become "martyrs" were offered great rewards in heaven. [47] As told in the *hadiths* (collection of verses attributed to Mohammed), martyrs will skip the period spent between the grave and judgment day and ascend straight to paradise where they will be attended by 72 black-eyed virgins.

Pious Muslims believed that a martyr didn't "die" but, instead, was "wed to the black-eyed in eternal paradise." Notices of the "departure" therefore, resembled wedding announcements rather than obituaries and the parents of martyrs (who were also accorded a special place in heaven along with other family members) were congratulated accordingly.

Along with the kudos (rather than condolences) bestowed by neighbors and friends, the families left behind after a martyr's mission had been completed were usually well-compensated monetarily by sponsoring organizations.

Potential martyrs were stirred by these shows of admiration and drew inspiration from circulated videos recording martyrs' ritualistic last testaments filmed just before a mission was carried out. For some, martyrdom was the most glorious way to escape the oppressive, poverty-stricken life they experienced in squalid refugee camps. For others (at least two of the bombers came from well-to-do families and many others were educated with good careers), it was an expression of piety, nationalism, defiance or warfare.

As a political tool, human bombs were especially effective because of the low cost of construction (an average bomb can cost only about $150 in materials) and reliability. Unlike timed devices, explosive-clad warriors could make last-minute changes to affect the greatest damage without being concerned with an escape plan.

The guaranteed media coverage of such attacks also helped instill a paralyzing fear in the populace that reached beyond the immediate victims and their families and forced the "oppressors" to address the demands of the "oppressed." It

---

[47] Mohammed, the founder of Islam said "a drop of blood shed in the cause of Allah, a night spent in arms, is of more avail than two months of fasting or prayer: whosoever falls in battle, his sins are forgiven, and at the day of judgement his limbs shall be supplied by the wings of angels and cherubim.

offered the Palestinians a degree of superiority over the Israeli military that could never be achieved through conventional warfare and drained the enemy's economic resources as they tried to defend themselves against the guerrillas. Shopkeepers, for instance, were forced to hire armed guards to prevent bombers from targeting their stores and the Israeli government paid heavily for security stations at border crossings. In May, 2002, the Israeli government also began to construct a fence along the *green line* (pre-1967) borders with the West Bank at a cost of millions of dollars to prevent infiltration by militant Palestinians.

Critics

Some Muslim and Palestinian critics of the human bombs employed by militant groups, Hamas, Islamic Jihad and the secular Al-Aqsa Martyrs Brigade among others, argued that the bombings defamed Islam for political use and were doing more to harm the Palestinians than help them. Muslim critics (including Sheik Abdul Aziz bin Abdullah al Sheik, the supreme religious leader of Saudi Arabia) claimed that these attacks contradicted the Quranic verse that instructed that "he who kills a human being without the latter being guilty of killing another or being guilty of spreading disorder in the land should be looked upon as if he had killed all mankind" (Quran 5:32). Moreover, harming innocent bystanders (especially women, children and the elderly), even in times of war, was forbidden by the Prophet Mohammed.

Many Palestinians also despaired that the attacks took them further away from normalized relations with the Jewish nation of Israel and the world.

Palestine in a Nutshell

AL-AQSA INTIFADA

In 1990, Iraqi president **Saddam Hussein** decided to invade the small country of Kuwait on Iraq's southern border. His aggressive act was countered by a U.S.-led coalition of 34 states which led to the 1991 Persian Gulf War.

By likening Iraq's "liberation" of Kuwait to the Palestinian goal of "liberating" Palestine, Hussein retained the support of PLO Chairman **Yasser Arafat**. Almost all other Arab nations, however, joined the western coalition in condemning Hussein's assault.

In order to maintain harmony among the mixed Arab and Western allies, the United States advised Israel to stay out of the conflict and to hold back retaliatory fire -- even when under attack by Iraqi scud missiles fired at Tel Aviv. By targeting Israel, Saddam Hussein hoped to draw the Jewish nation into the war thereby turning Iraq's conquest of Kuwait into a greater Israeli-Arab conflict and forcing the Arab states to shift their allegiance from the Western alliance to the Iraqi side. But with Israel's restraint, the coalition remained intact and Iraq was compelled to withdraw from Kuwait defeated.

The Gulf War only lasted a few days but the repercussions had a tremendous impact on Israel, the Palestinians and the West. Israel became aware of its vulnerability to attacks from Arab nations farther afield than its immediate neighbors. Europe and the United States recognized the deep implications of the continuing Israeli-Arab conflict. And Arafat's ill-fated alliance with Hussein alienated the Palestinians from their wealthy Gulf state benefactors.

With the Palestinians seemingly having supported the "wrong side" in the Gulf crisis, international opinion swung in favor of the Israelis after the war. As compensation for the damage caused by the Iraqi scud missiles, Israel won generous grants and loan guarantees from the U.S. and was given virtual *carte-blanche* in its dealings against the Palestinians They imposed round-the-clock curfews in some areas during the war, for example, and Palestinian movement within Israel was severely restricted.

Meanwhile, in retribution for supporting the Iraqi dictator, the Gulf states cut off all charitable contributions to Palestine and half a million workers employed in the Gulf region (whose income accounted for 8% of the Palestinian gross national product) were expelled.

Combined, these circumstances made the post-Gulf War period an opportune time to launch peace talks.

The resultant **Madrid** peace initiative and, more significantly, the diplomatic peace process being conducted in **Oslo** in 1993 (see "Peace Treaties" in Israel

section) gave hope to Palestinians and Israelis alike that a resolution to the Middle East crisis was close at hand. The demonstrations, commercial strikes, tax-resistance and stone-throwing came to a halt marking the official end of the 1987 *intifada*. For the Palestinians, the peace treaties heralded the prospect of an end to Israel's occupation, the creation of a Palestinian state and the easing of restrictions and daily inconveniences. But these expectations were dashed several years later.

After seven years of negotiations, the Palestinians still didn't have an independent state and the Israeli settler population in the West Bank, Gaza Strip and East Jerusalem had doubled. None of the most pressing issues -- the status of Palestinian refugees, control of Jerusalem, distribution of water resources and permanent borders -- had been dealt with (all were relegated to "final status" talks that never occurred), and the living standard in the Palestinian areas had deteriorated to unbearable depths.

With the unrestricted construction of Jewish settlements on Palestinian land, furthermore, came a proliferation of security checkpoints that made it increasingly difficult for Palestinians to get to their jobs or attend school. In addition, the Israelis cut down tens of thousands of olive and fruit trees (grown by Palestinian farmers who relied on the fruits for their livelihood) in order to make room for bypass roads built to connect the Israeli settlements to one another. The roads, which dissected Palestinian territory, also carved the land into isolated pockets of Palestinian communities.

Adding to the discontent, unemployment in Palestinian territory had reached 40% and Israeli-imposed discriminatory policies resulted in cutbacks in water quotas supplying millions of Palestinians.

Under the pressure of substandard living conditions, humiliating treatment by Israeli soldiers and the frustration over the failure of the peace treaties to ameliorate the situation, the Palestinians were on the brink of revolt. All that was needed was a trigger to set off the discontented population and that trigger came on September 28, 2000.

On that day, then-Defense Minister **Ariel Sharon** decided to visit the **Haram al-Sharif** (Noble Sanctuary) accompanied by a thousand Israeli police officers. The incident was a grave insult to the Palestinians who interpreted his provocative move as a demonstration of Jewish sovereignty over the compound.

Sharon's visit was immediately met by angry demonstrations played out in the same manner as the 1987 *intifada*. But the Israeli response this time around was much more brutal. Live fire replaced rubber bullets and gunships and F-16 bombers were used to repel the Palestinian rebels. Curfews and other collective punishments were imposed on Palestinian cities for long periods of time virtu-

ally imprisoning people in their homes.

The Palestinians, in turn, responded by deploying their new Palestinian police and security forces armed with Kalashnikov rifles and unleashing the Al-Aqsa Martyrs Brigade.

Al-Aqsa Martyrs Brigade

Soon after the eruption of the al-Aqsa *intifada* (as the uprising following Ariel Sharon's visit to the Al-Aqsa Mosque was called), a group of radical activists affiliated with Yasser Arafat's Fatah faction of the PLO emerged as the Al-Aqsa Martyrs Brigade. Although the organization was rooted in Palestinian nationalism rather than Islamic fundamentalism (as were its militant counterparts, Hamas and Islamic Jihad), the Al-Aqsa Brigade drew on Islamic ideals to inspire its members in their struggle to establish a Palestinian state with Jerusalem as its capital.

Initially, this militant offshoot of the Fatah movement vowed only to target Israeli soldiers and settlers in the West Bank and Gaza Strip. After the assassination of the group's West bank leader, **Raed Karmi**, in January 2002, and in response to the rising death toll of Palestinians at the hands of the Israelis, the group expanded its battlefield to include civilian targets. The Brigade, which was the first to employ female martyrs, began a spree of attacks in early 2002 that took more Israeli lives than both Hamas and Islamic Jihad and had earned it a designation as a Foreign Terrorist Organization (FTO) by the U.S. State Department in March of that year.

The organizations' close relationship to Arafat's Fatah faction has led to speculation that the Palestinian Authority president was supporting the militant group ideologically and financially and perhaps even orchestrated its activities. While some of the group's leaders admit that they did not receive instructions from Arafat, others claimed that the group acted independently. Arafat's advisers said that he did not control the Brigade while Israeli officials claimed to have proof that Arafat was directly involved in Al-Aqsa's militant activity and that he, therefore, should be condemned as a terrorist.

ISSUES

Refugees

Two years before Ben-Gurion declared the independence of the state of Israel (an event labeled al-Nakbah or "the catastrophe" by Arabs), more than a million Palestinians lived in the territory that would later be absorbed into the borders of the new Jewish state. By 1948, their number had dropped to 150,000.

In the course of the Arab-Israeli war that followed Israel's creation, hundreds of thousands of Palestinians fled the territory to avoid the fighting and to escape the threat of ethnic cleansing by Israeli militants (the massacre of Palestinians living in the village of **Deir Yassin** was upheld as an example of potential Israeli brutality). Others were ordered to leave by the Israelis or persuaded to evacuate by Arabs who promised that they would return victorious once the Zionists had been defeated. Nearly all the Palestinians, many clutching the keys to their houses,[48] expected the war to last just a few weeks and that their return would be imminent.

Wealthy Palestinians checked into hotels or took out short leases on apartments. Others moved in with friends and relatives living abroad. The vast majority, however, were forced to move into temporary tent shelters built across the border.

By the fall of 1948, the flood of Palestinian refugees had reached a dangerous level compelling the United Nations to establish the **United Nations Relief for Palestinian Refugees (UNRPR)** and later the **United Nations Relief and Works Agency (UNRWA)** to provide food, medicine, housing and education to the impoverished refugees. In response to the crisis, in December 1948 the United Nations also passed **Resolution 194** stating that *refugees wishing to return to their homes and live at peace with their neighbors should be permitted to do so at the earliest practicable date and compensation should be paid for the property of those choosing not to return and for loss of or damage to property.*

Regardless of the terms of U.N. Resolution 194 and in violation of Article 13 of the 1948 **Universal Declaration of Human Rights** (which declared that *everyone has the right to leave any country, including his own, and to return to his country*) and Article 49 of the **Fourth Geneva Convention** of 1950 (which stipulated that *persons [evacuated by an occupying power] shall be transferred back to their homes as soon as hostilities in the area in question have ceased*), Israel did not allow the Palestinian refugees to return to their homes.

Today the number of displaced Palestinians (the refugees and their descendants) has been estimated to number about five million worldwide with three million living in the West Bank, Gaza Strip and neighboring Arab countries. More that a million Palestinians are believed to still be living in the 59 UN-operated refugee camps.

---

[48] The key has become a symbol of Palestinian refugee rights. Half a century later, some refugees still cling to their house keys in anticipation of the day that they will be permitted to return home.

Palestine in a Nutshell

While the repatriation of all the Palestinians to their former homes may be technically impractical, Israel's acknowledgment of the rights of refugees to return to their former homes (and hence admission of responsibility for the crisis) remains a passionate matter of principle to the Palestinian population. [49]

Settlements

One of the greatest obstacles to peace and potentially the biggest impediment blocking the creation of an independent Palestinian state remains Israel's continual practice of settling Jews in Palestinian-populated areas.

In the same fashion as the Zionists in Palestine during the Ottoman period, the Israelis used a number of "legal" methods since 1948 to acquire land that had once belonged to Palestinians. By declaring that sections of territory were registered to the state, for instance, land (whether populated or not) could be "legally" confiscated and returned to Israel. Palestinian residents who objected were required to present sufficient documentation (often hard to come by) to prove that they were the rightful owners.

Israel's **Absentee Property Law** enacted in 1950 gave Israelis the right to acquire property that had been "abandoned" by those who had been expelled from their homes or fled voluntarily. The **Land Ordinance of 1943** also authorized the Israeli government to confiscate land for "public purposes," and **Israel's Defense Regulation 125** (1945) allowed Israelis to declare areas "closed for security reasons." Entire villages could be evacuated under these ordinances, opening the way for further Jewish settlement.

Once the land had been secured, the Israeli government established outposts, --that is, small pieces of land earmarked for state purposes (as a site for a telephone antenna, for example, a scientific research site, a water tower, an industrial park etc.). Slowly the outposts expanded into small villages colonized by settlers lured by government grants, loans, low rents, cheap property, reductions in taxes and other incentives.

After the communities had been established, schools, shops and government offices would be built to accommodate the new residents and soldiers would be posted around the settlements for security.

To date, Israel has established more than 150 settlements in Palestinian territories (**Peace Now**, an Israel advocacy group, counted the construction of over 60 outposts since **Ariel Sharon** came to office in March, 2001) housing more than 300,000 Jewish settlers -- all in violation of international law and breaching the tenets of the Road Map for Peace plan.

Israel has consistently contravened **Article 49** of the **Geneva Convention** in 1949, which states that *an occupying power shall not deport or transfer parts of its own civilian population into the territory it occupies,* and violated the **Hague Regulations** which prohibit an occupying power to undertake permanent

---

[49] Since 1976, Palestinians have annually marked March 30th (Land Day) as a day of resistance to protest Israel's land seizures in 1948 and in objection to unresolved claims to housing and property restitution.

changes in the occupied area.

Israel has also failed to abide by the policies of the 2002 **Road Map for Peace** which called on Israel to dismantle unauthorized settler outposts and stop the expansion of established settlements. Ariel Sharon, one of the strongest proponents of the settler movement reportedly confessed that his government would not curtail the expansion of settlements nor dismantle the Jewish neighborhoods. In fact, in the first half of 2003, the number of settlers in Palestinian territories actually increased by thousands.

Even if Sharon had been willing to fulfill the tenets of the road map, the prime minister would be countered by members of one of Israel's most powerful parties, **Likud**, which held (and still holds) as its platform that *the Jewish communities in Judea, Samaria (the West Bank) and Gaza are the realization of Zionists values. Settlement of the land is a clear expression of the unassailable right of the Jewish people to the Land of Israel and constitutes an important asset in the defense of the vital interests of the State of Israel. The Likud will continue to strengthen and develop these communities and will prevent their uprooting.*

Along with providing the Israelis "**facts on the ground**" and an excuse to maintain a military presence within the Palestinian communities, the settlements also helped thwart Palestinian ambitions of creating an independent state in the West Bank and Gaza Strip. By scattering the settlements strategically among the Palestinian cities, the Jewish neighborhoods separated the Palestinians communities into isolated pockets giving the area a Swiss cheese appearance. By partitioning the land this way and hindering geographic continuity, the Israelis were making it nearly impossible to create an integrated Palestinian state. Bypass roads connecting the settlements with Israel proper further divided the territory.

Al-Quds (Jerusalem)

It is no coincidence that the site of **Haram al-Sharif** (also called the Noble Sanctuary or Temple Mount) is considered holy to both Muslims and Jews. As a site once visited by the prophets Abraham, Moses, Jesus and other biblical figures, its spiritual significance holds as much weight to the Muslims as it does to Jews and Christians. It is written in the Quran (sura 12:1) that Mohammed, himself, made a trip to Jerusalem in the seventh century during a "night journey" led by the angel Gabriel. From the holy site, Mohammed was transported to heaven where he met the prophets who had come before him and received commandments for the faithful (see "Islam").

To commemorate the event, **Caliph Abdel Malik ibn Marwan** (founder of the Umayyad dynasty) erected the **Dome of the Rock** over the platform from where Mohammed had taken his first step into paradise. In A.D. 715, the Umayyads also built the **al-Aqsa** ("furthest") **Mosque** near the Dome of the Rock to serve as a meeting place for pilgrims who visited from around the Muslim world. The city of Jerusalem became the third holiest destination to Muslims after the cities of Mecca and Medina and remained in Muslim hands for centuries.

The deep importance of Jerusalem to both the Muslims and Jews was also rec-

ognized by the United Nations prompting the organization to omit the city from 1947 plans to partition the land into Jewish and Muslim spheres of influence and putting the city, instead, under UN (that is, international) jurisdiction.

Haram al-Sharif/Temple Mount

A year later, though, the city was divided when Jordan won administrative control over the eastern half or "Old City" of Jerusalem (including the Noble Sanctuary) and Israel gained control over the western portion of Jerusalem (largely comprising the "new city").

With Israel's occupation of the West Bank in 1967, the city was again reunited under Israeli control. Immediately after the annexation, Israel attempted to secure its dominant position over the city by declaring Jerusalem the nation's capital,[50] expanding the municipal boundaries (Jerusalem grew from four square miles in 1967 to about 50 square miles) and constructing huge settlements that virtually cut off the Noble Sanctuary from Palestinian towns on the outskirts of Jerusalem.

Today the Palestinians claim Jerusalem as the capital of the Palestinian Authority based on the idea of "one city, two capitals" -- a plan that allows Israel to maintain a capital in the western portion of the city and the Palestinians to establish their capital in East Jerusalem.[51]

Old City, Jerusalem

- Muslim Quarter
- Christian Quarter
- Dome of the Rock
- Western/Wailing Wall
- Jewish Quarter
- Armenian Quarter

---

[50] Most countries in the world do not recognize Jerusalem as Israel's capital choosing instead to maintain their embassies in the city of Tel Aviv.

[51] Many Palestinians who had bought less expensive homes in Arab neighborhoods just outside Jerusalem began moving back to the city for fear that the separation wall under construction between Israeli and Palestinian territories would soon prevent them from visiting the city.